# Cape May H

## Elaine's Haunted Mansion and Other Eerie Beach Tales

D. P. Roseberry

with Psychic Laurie Hull

4880 Lower Valley Road  Atglen, Pennsylvania 19310

**Other Schiffer Books by D. P. Roseberry**
*Ghosts of Valley Forge and Phoenixville, 978-0-7643-2633-2, $14.95*

**Other Schiffer Books on Related Subjects**
Schiffer Publishing has a whole department devoted to the Paranormal, with several books
to go along with it. Some include:
*Haunted Richmond, 978-0-7643-2712-4, $14.95* and *Seance 101, 978-0-7643-2717-9, $19.95.*
For other great titles, visit Schifferbooks.com

Designed by John P. Cheek
Cover design by Bruce Waters
Type set in Casablanca Antique/New Baskerville BT

ISBN: 978-0-7643-2821-3
Printed in China

**Disclaimer and Acknowledgement of Trademarks**
The Ouija is a registered trademark of Parker Brother's Games.

Published by Schiffer Publishing Ltd.
4880 Lower Valley Road
Atglen, PA 19310
Phone: (610) 593-1777; Fax: (610) 593-2002
E-mail: Info@schifferbooks.com

For the largest selection of fine reference books on this and related subjects, please visit our
web site at **www.schifferbooks.com**
We are always looking for people to write books on new and related subjects. If you have an
idea for a book please contact us at the above address.

This book may be purchased from the publisher.
Include $3.95 for shipping.
Please try your bookstore first.
You may write for a free catalog.

In Europe, Schiffer books are distributed by
Bushwood Books
6 Marksbury Ave.
Kew Gardens
Surrey TW9 4JF England
Phone: 44 (0) 20 8392-8585; Fax: 44 (0) 20 8392-9876
E-mail: info@bushwoodbooks.co.uk
Website: www.bushwoodbooks.co.uk
Free postage in the U.K., Europe; air mail at cost.

# Dedication

*In memory of George and J.C.: two reasons that I continue to believe in ghosts.*

*Also to my husband, Carroll, who continues to beg me not to bring ghosts home, and to my daughter, Angela, who always knew I was strange in a ghostly kind of way. My parents deserve some credit here as well. It was them—particularly my father—who passed on the love of the paranormal, usually in front of the television set watching Saturday Night's Chiller Theater when I was still too young to know that the fantasy on the little screen was an actuality in the "real world." (And of course, my mother who tolerated our behavior! She's now my best fan!)*

# Acknowledgments

I've had the opportunity to work with many paranormal researchers over the past months and have been amazed at the wonderful "spirit" of cooperation that takes place routinely among and between these groups of feisty people. Yes, I've heard of the turf wars in the world of ghost hunting, but more and more, these kind, energetic, and very serious researchers have begun the journey toward combined collaboration when it comes to scoping out ghosts around the country and sharing the results of their investigations with each other—and me. Whether I'm talking to hunters in Colorado, psychics in North Carolina, or researchers and sensitizes right here in my current home state of Pennsylvania, I've seen the fine lines of turf smudged and then removed entirely. State and city borderlines seem to have evaporated.

This has been especially true in the research of this book about the lovely Cape May, New Jersey. Laurie Hull, Director of the Delaware County Paranormal Research group in Pennsylvania has always had a special place in her heart for this quaint beach community. As a ghost investigator, sensitive, and author, she was quick to step forward to offer her talent after hearing that I was planning to write a contemporary book about the ghosts of Cape May. Not only did she talk with me about ten of the wonderful bed and breakfast inns of this lovely town, but volunteered to guide me through the varied haunts to provide "sensitive" data. (It's wonderful to hear the first-hand accounts of ghostly activity, but quite another to have someone along who can interact with spirits as they approach!)

Further, Ron Long of Elaine's Haunted Mansion Restaurant, Dinner Theater, and Walking Ghost Tour was kind enough to open the doors to me (twice!) and showed great respect of the author process—always a plus when interviewing!

Thanks also goes to all the wonderful businesses and people of Cape May who welcomed me in my quest.

There is, of course, my very professional and educated home group, the Chester County Paranormal Research Society, who provide me with stories, glossary material, equipment descriptions for ghost hunting for the book, and continue my ongoing investigative training.

Thanks to Schiffer author Fiona Broome (*Ghosts of Austin, Texas*) for "Fiona's Tips for Taking Great Ghost Photos" and "Top Ten Places to Find Ghosts" and

Schiffer author Scott Lefebvre (*Spooky and Creepy Long Island*) for the "Guide for Urban Exploration."

Additionally, a special thanks to Tina Skinner for valued interviews and photographs with Cape May folks early on, and for mentoring me through the ghost-writing process; and Elwood "Woody" Koch for allowing me to use some of his postcards from his wonderful collection of Cape May history.

My husband also deserves thanks for providing me with some lovely photographs and for allowing me to drag him around to all the special haunts of Cape May.

# Contents

*Acknowledgements* .............................................. 9

*Introduction* ...................................................... 15

*Chapter One: Welcome to Elaine's*
Elaine's Haunted Mansion Restaurant,
Victorian Inn Bed and Breakfast, Dinner
Theater and Walking Ghost Tour ...................27

*Chapter Two:*
The Southern Mansion .................................103

*Chapter Three:*
Windward House Bed and Breakfast Inn.......111

*Chapter Four:*
The Queen Victoria® Bed & Breakfast Inn......119

*Chapter Five:*
The Inn at 22 Jackson Street ........................127

*Chapter Six:*
Congress Hall.................................................137

*Chapter Seven:*
The Macomber Hotel.....................................149

*Chapter Eight:*
Cabanna's Beach Bar and Grill......................157

**Chapter Nine: Quickie Cape May Haunts**
Atlantic Book Store ...................................... 165
The Peter Shields Inn .................................... 167
The John F. Craig House ................................ 170
The Thorn and the Rose ................................ 172
The Washington Inn ..................................... 175
The Columns by the Sea ................................ 177
The Victorian Lace Inn .................................. 179
**Chapter Ten: Other Creepy Places!**
The Cape May Puffin .................................... 181
The Angel of the Sea .................................... 182
Poverty Beach ............................................ 182
The Brass Bed Inn ....................................... 182
The Witches League of Cape May ................... 183
**Chapter Eleven: On the Beaches of Cape May**
Higbee Beach ............................................. 185
The Cape May Light House ............................ 189
The Cape May Point Bunker ........................... 193
Anyplace on the Beaches of Cape May ........... 195
**Chapter Twelve:**
Thoughts of Psychic Laurie Hull .................. 197
**Bibliography and Resource List** .................... 205
**Appendix**
*Fiona's Tips for Taking Great Ghost Photos* .. 207
*Guide for Urban Exploration* ................... 209
*Glossary* ..................................... 213
*Equipment* ................................... 217

# Foreword

Since the writing of my first ghost book, *Ghosts of Valley Forge and Phoenixville* (Pennsylvania), I've learned quite a bit about ghosts and my beliefs in them. Don't get me wrong; I've always believed in ghosts, but I'd never actually witnessed, nor had I been a part of, a truly haunting experience that left me with wide eyes. I'd had experiences with Ouigi Boards (boo-hiss-not-a-good-thing-beware), invisible angelic beings who kept me from harm or who pointed the way in times of stress, and "sensations" that have creeped me out on more than one occasion. But once I began research on ghostly activities and places and became involved with others who were like-minded—opening myself up to the worlds beyond…well, then I developed a much more haunted perception on the subject—and everything related to it. Though an amateur in ghost research still, I'm no longer inexperienced.

From the outside looking in, one might laugh at my limited knowledge. I've been warned not to bring ghosts home to haunt my own house (or those dearest to me), to keep them to myself in the office (people hate it when their computers are mysteriously turned on or off and lights flicker), and to consider checking into the local asylum for at least a weekend or two. All in good fun, right? But fun or not, since I've become involved routinely in the paranormal, I've had to:

• Consider buying a new pair of glasses for not believing that Revolutionary cemetery's ghosts were scratching people while they were inside the cemetery walls (read about this encounter in my Ghosts of Valley Forge and Phoenixville book),

• Calm my heart from a smoke alarm warning that spanned two states for a warning from beyond about my daughter's safety (I may never be able to be composed enough to write about this one—we'll see),

• Cry my way through a séance (don't ask),

• Marvel at being overcome with an energy of despair at a famous Pennsylvania prison (read about it in the upcoming Philadelphia Ghosts);

• And witness a flying library book (the Phoenixville Public Library—also in Ghosts of Valley Forge and Phoenixville).

These kinds of things, though they may sound trivial here, tend to make a regular believer *more* of a believer! And maybe even a ghostly fanatic.

As I've become involved with true paranormal researchers, like the Chester County Paranormal Research Society, I've found that people I've come into contact with look at ghostly activities in many differ-ent ways. Researchers can very nearly always be called debunkers because they are so careful to rule out any possibility of inaccuracy. Feeling it necessary to prove certain activity *not* ghostly helps them prove the *reality* of ghosts. They check electricity in areas investigated, they plot floor plans by using graphs, they take scientific readings—they leave no tombstone unturned.

Before being exposed to researchers, my expe-rience with ghosts had more to do with campfires and tales passed from one person to the next. Oh, and maybe a movie or two in the dead of the night. *Things* didn't happen to me in any physical sense that I could grasp—beyond my own little perceptions and incidences of, what I would consider, a minor intuitive nature. But once someone begins to see manifesta-tions of the mystical, the whole concept of certainty changes. *How does it change?* Stories and tales told by those experiencing paranormal activity no longer sit on the back burner of belief once you've seen real ghostly activity up close and personal. *Now…* when I hear stories, I have a different mindset. I might now ask specific questions to gauge their surroundings or try to ascertain things that might be caused by normal circumstances—as opposed to paranormal. (Is it air conditioning or a ghostly cold spot? Whispered voices or ghostly chat? Perception or reality?)

The difference is that nowadays I *believe* first; then consider the facts; and finally reflect on a conclusion.

Previously, the entire thinking process would have been reversed. My first thought might have been: *"That's nonsense. Can't happen."* Followed by the facts: *"I saw a rose move inside a vase when there was no air movement to move it"* (see my *Valley Forge* book for this strange event). And finally, I *believe* what I saw.

I suppose what I'm saying is: ghosts are real—and it looks like they're here to stay.

So think twice as you stroll the streets of Cape May. You never know who may be just outside your reality and walking right beside you. For Cape May, my friends, is truly haunted. Trust me on this.

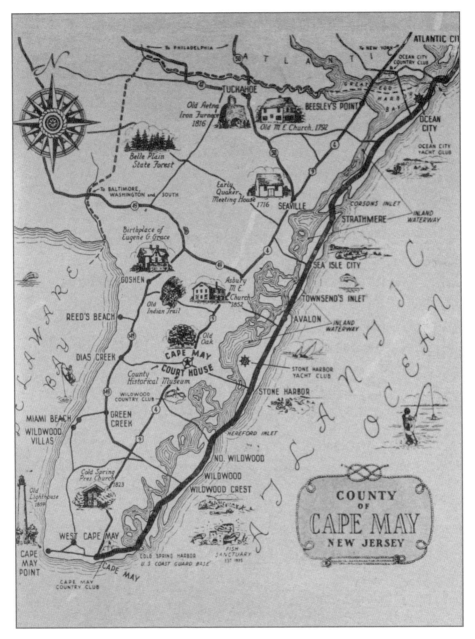

A circa 1930s postcard map detailing "The New Ocean Drive from Cape May, New Jersey to Atlantic City, New Jersey." For some, a ghostly drive... *Postcard courtesy of the Elwood "Woody" Koch collection.*

# Introduction

## On the Way to Beautiful Cape May

Anyone who has ever been to beautiful Cape May, New Jersey, is aware of the gorgeous beaches, magnificent Victorian architecture, and friendly people that invite the rest-and-relaxation-seeking vacationers to its shores to unwind—or wind up—year after year. Nestled at the southern tip of New Jersey, this historic town was known as the "Queen of the Seaside Resorts" (before Atlantic City spirited that title away) for good reason. Some of the most lovely vacation spots and living quarters in the nation can be found in this thriving resort town.

But with the excitement, the history, the architecture, and the splendor of the ocean and all its marvelous offerings, also come the hauntings—the ghostly presences that wander just the other side of our reality. Yes, Cape May is certainly haunted. Renowned investigators, like Craig McManus, and specialty research groups, like the Delaware County

Paranormal Ghosts Research and the Haunted
New Jersey (as well as other prominent individuals), have been among those making the rounds
in Cape May, proclaiming that ghosts do, indeed,
inhabit this seaside community—right alongside
the living.

But where do these lost souls come from? Some
come from historic events that mark cities and towns
around the world in the days of nature turning
against man.

Cape May began to develop the reputation as
American's oldest seaside resort as early as the mid-
1700s, spurred by the economics of those who came
to use it as a port taking wares to the thriving Philadelphia docks and then outward into the world.

Whether it was timber or agriculture, peacetime
or war, Cape May was drawing people to its land—
and benefiting from the exposure. This pattern,
ever-changing through the years, but still reaching
out, led to positive economic development, including
a boom in tourism.

Early on, Cape May's hotels, particularly, were
huge and wooden—the perfect target for fire in a
time when flames were not easy to extinguish. In
the 1870s, a fire of great magnitude destroyed the
town, burning hotels and homes alike all the way to
the ground. Smaller wood-frame cottages appeared
in the wake of the disaster for a time; and there was
a lot of rebuilding over the years. But now, the hotel

guests who might have moved from hotel to rebuilt hotel in a previous era, seem to linger still—in places that no longer entirely resemble the yesteryear dwellings. Only now, they linger in another form—an eerie form.

Though the draw of the crowds through the years seemed to point to a need for the modernized resorts and hotels that were cropping up in Atlantic City and in the Wildwoods, Cape May was determined to hold onto their ghosts—I mean, old Victorian architecture. They held out for the warm charm of history, and finally were able to renovate and reopen some of the previously run-down buildings as spectacular bed-and-breakfast inns, shops, restaurants, and other varied "haunts." Cape May was even awarded a designation as a National Historic Landmark City. The town was serving a new kind of population as people were beginning to recognize the attractive idea of walking, of small-town atmosphere, of timeless seaside magic. So, while it held onto its charm, Cape May had also developed and maintained a fertile ground for ghosts.

But ghosts do not arise only from historic rubble. New and old buildings, places, and people have haunts. Some research has shown that, oftentimes, a single person will attract ghostly activity, or be aware of it, when those around them experience nothing. And ghosts are not an uncommon entity on the many beaches of New Jersey, either.

In fact, on the way to Cape May, here's a chilling account of a ghostly New Jersey beach that might serve as a beginning for your haunted expedition. It just might entice you to travel Jersey's coastline to visit this not-so-quiet little beach town of Cape May—or not, depending on your fear factor.

A circa 1920s beach scene (west of Cox's Pier). More than sunbathers visit beautiful Cape May—it's also a place for those open to the paranormal. *Postcard courtesy of the Elwood "Woody" Koch collection*

### ...And So the Scares Begin...

Jill, Russell, and Jason were good friends, and it was in their minds to enjoy the beautiful sandy beaches of the Jersey shores—to get away from the hustle and bustle of the city, traffic, and busy work and school-day schedules. Renting a beach house was a wonderful idea—a time to relax and enjoy some fun in the sun during the lazy summer. Finding just what they were looking for in a small beach cottage in a typical New Jersey beach town about two houses away from the beach, they, and a few of their friends, settled in for a fun-filled weekend at the shore.

But, as things will often go in ghost stories and haunts, not all was to be fun and peaceful for very long.

Jason, a tall, thin high school track star, brought his Ouigi Board. Jill knew—or at least suspected—that this was not a good thing from the very beginning. She'd heard the warnings from others. But she was the type of person who held onto her opinions and remained securely on the fence of fear until proof was given that she should fall to one side or another of certainty. She really didn't know for a *fact* that the Ouigi was dangerous. It could be just a toy. Either way, it certainly was not something to become upset about—no need to throw a wrench into their lazy evenings on the beach with fears of goblins and ghosts.

The day had turned into a clear, beautiful night when Jill's girlfriends took off to do some shopping and to generally traipse about the beach town doing "girly things." She had not wanted to go with them, opting to stay around the house with the guys.

It was around midnight when the "fun" began for the three friends who were left to their own entertainment. With a bottle of wine, a couple glasses, and Ouigi Board in tow, the three walked out to the beach, to spend some time beneath the stars and to hear the surf rolling quietly into shore. After a glass of wine (only one or two), they pulled out the Ouigi Board.

For those unfamiliar with this popular and often-times fun "game," it is comprised basically of a board covered with the letters of the alphabet, the numbers *0* through *9*, and the words *yes, no,* and *maybe,* that allow a planchette (a triangular little device held up by two casters and a vertical pointer that, when lightly touched by two sets of fingertips, spells out messages that can be seen letter by letter through a clear round opening on the top of the triangle) to tell the future, past, or present to those touching it. The three friends began to play with it by asking questions, but the board did not respond right away.

Finally annoyed and about to give up, they asked in agitation, "Is there anyone there who wants to talk with us?"

It was then that Jason felt the first trembling of a ghostly experience—and it wasn't pleasant. He began to get very sick to his stomach; full-blown flu sick, in fact. (This, by the way, is a common reaction to the supernatural for some folks.) The three friends dismissed this—even Jason—as they continued asking the board questions.

The Ouigi, now, was becoming more interesting; or more frightening depending upon your point of view. It kept spelling out words:

*I am here.*

They would ask, "Who is here?"

*I am.*

There was something...scary...about the responses that were repeated over and over again. It went beyond the everyday-fun-replies that have been known to come from such devices. A shiver crept down Jill's spine. Somehow, she knew that the entity behind the board was not a pleasant creature.

The planchette on the Ouigi continued to move faster and faster…

*I am here. I am here. I am here.*

The three continued to try to find out *who* was there, answering each *I am here* with a *Who is here?* question. Finally the letters spelled out:

*H A T E*

This puzzled them. It was not an answer to their question, but it was definitely another line of thought from this *being from beyond*. They questioned: *Hate who?*

The board moved very fast now and Jill began to think that the other two young men were playing on her emotions by moving the planchette to scare her.

She called them on it. "Stop foolin' around," she snapped. "You're scaring me."

They, of course, denied that they were doing any-thing to move the gadget (which is often the case in Ouigi Board incidents). They asked again: *Hate who?* The board sat still for a few seconds and then began to spell over and over again:

*H E R    H E R    H E R    H E R*

Jill sucked in her breath, no longer noticing the calm waters and the warm night around her. *Her.* Was the thing from beyond talking about *her*? There cer-tainly was no other "her" with them…

Russell and Jason were thinking the same thing. They asked, "Who? The one who is sitting here with us?"

There was an immediate response.

*YES   YES   YES   YES   YES*

The planchette was nearly jumping and sliding off the board, the talker was so excited to tell them that Jill was the cursed *her*. Jill was distraught now and she no longer wanted to play with the Ouigi. Scenarios were going through her head. The best case scenario was that her friends were moving the planchette and having some fun at her expense. The worst? Well, that was another story and much more frightening, since she had no idea why someone from the other side would hate her with such vehemence.

It is customary in Ouigi Board etiquette (if indeed there is such a thing) to say *Hello* when starting and *Goodbye* when finishing board usage. It's been said that in this way the pathway to the world beyond is opened and closed. Others say that opening is easier than closing, and that the "goodbye" theory does not work. The truth of the situation is not really known. (Something for us to ponder…)

However, Jill, who was one who played by the rules in most cases, decided that enough was enough of this mean-spirited Ouigi talker. "Goodbye," she said to the board, giving the planchette a physical nudge towards the same word.

In fast movement, the planchette rushed to the word *no*, leaving the word to circle in a spherical motion and then returning to *no* time and time again. It would then start to spell the word *hate*, over and over.

"This is insane!" said Jill, pulling her hands from the planchette. She looked over at Jason and saw that he was getting sicker and sicker—his face held a greenish tint from nausea. She pushed the planchette to the word *goodbye* and shouted it at the same time to the board before throwing it down into the sand.

Jason suddenly jumped up and took off running up the beach as fast as he could. Russell was close behind. Jill, not knowing why they were running, but certainly not to be left behind, began to run as well; but as she closed the gap between her and the young men, almost to the top of a big dune, she felt a slamming blow to her upper back. The force was so great that it knocked her face-first into the sand.

Horrified, she called out, "Russell, Jason, I fell!"

Russell stopped and turned to help her, but stood routed in place. Looking up and over her shoulder, he gasped—at something—and then just turned and ran.

Jill did not know what he saw behind her and was afraid to look—very afraid. She knew that she just had to get up and run as the boys had. But again she was pushed down into the sand by a forceful hand at her back. Fighting her fright, she scrambled up and ran without looking back until she got to the beach house.

Standing in front of the house on the street, the three friends just looked at each other with wide eyes, no one saying a word. They didn't know what to say, so they said nothing.

Sometime later, when Jill told her story to her husband, she was told that the beach was very haunted and that many people had experienced angry manifestations there. The tale told is that of a pretty young girl caught in the middle of a love triangle. When her love did not show one night as she waited for him on the beach, the young woman could not fight off the anger and despair that her intended might never come to her—she committed suicide in that area of the sands.

These three innocent beach goers had invited an angry spirit into their world through the Ouigi Board. But who was that spirit and why did it hate Jill so much? Was it the angry girl who felt Jill was a threat to her beloved? Was it the girl's lover, angry that his love had left him behind by committing suicide? Or was something else evil on that beach?

After this experience, Jill advised me that her life has been opened to many more paranormal experiences. She believes that the energy and karma available to spirits is more evident once that door to the mind has been opened. "Spirits know who is receptive and who isn't," she said candidly.

So join me as we travel down the coast of New Jersey to the seaside treasure, Cape May. There are those who have been waiting a long time for you...

# Chapter One
# Welcome to Elaine's

*Haunted Mansion Restaurant & Dinner Theater,*
*Victorian Inn Bed & Breakfast, Walking Ghost Tour*

513 Lafayette Street
Cape May, NJ 08204
609-884-4358
http://www.elainesdinnertheater.com

---

Directions: Take Garden State Parkway South (it becomes NJ 109 South). NJ 109 becomes Lafayette Street. Follow to 513 Lafayette on the right side.

---

Ghostly Aspects:

- Sounds of footsteps, people talking
- Laughter of children
- Crying, voices calling out
- Orb Activity
- Feathers
- Cold Spots
- Visual sightings (Cats, People)
- Eerie feelings
  (Tingling, goose flesh, lightheadedness)
- Shadows
- EMF and EVP readings
- Strange antique clothing
- Batteries drained
- Sounds of moving objects
- Heavy air quality
- Air movement
- Floral smells

The beautiful Elaine's Haunted Mansion (Restaurant, Bed and Breakfast, Dinner Theater, and Walking Ghost Tour). This photo was taken from across the street—where the Catholic school is located. School kids first noticed the second floor ghost many, many years ago--beginning what was thought of initially as a legend. We now know that this haunting is not a legend, but reality.

## ...Could it be...

The nurse stood on the second floor balcony watching the Irish servant in the garden. The garden was a lovely place of retreat for everyone at the home—especially for the child. Emmy, even at her youthful age, loved to sit among the flowers and watch the buzzing bees taking their sweet nectar from plant to plant.

Emmy was under the weather this day. So though the sun shone brightly, the nurse's own heart felt dark and gloomy—for that was the sentiment she held whenever the youngster took to her bed with the weakness.

She'd come to the summer home in Cape May as Emily Read's caretaker by predestined luck, it seemed. The good and kind Dr. Read from Philadelphia had been a friend of her family and knew of her knack with children and her abilities as a caretaker. After all, hadn't she taken care of her ailing mother all those years? And her own younger sister? She'd been perfect for the position.

Still, she hadn't planned on the emotional attachment and despair she felt whenever the child was weakened in body or spirit—which, due to her illness, was most of the time. It wasn't that Emmy needed carrying from place to place, or that she could not run and jump and play like others her age; it was the quiet bravery she saw in the child. This was a bravery that she'd never felt for herself. Emmy was a survivor, and the nurse felt sure that her survival would last forever. And, that for as long as she was able to love little Emmy, her own endurance would meet the ages, right alongside the child.

The nurse stood on the second floor balcony looking out to the garden...

## My First Visit to Elaine's

I went, initially, to Elaine's Haunted Mansion with more or less an early fact-finding mission in mind. I'd been visiting a few of the bed and breakfasts in Cape May, seeking ghosts and ghostly stories, and wanted to end the day at Elaine's. It was to be a wind-down time for me, because Elaine's and I have history together.

Some years ago—and I'd not been back since—my husband and I became engaged at Elaine's Haunted Mansion Restaurant. For those of you wondering, why in the world would anyone want to become engaged at a haunted restaurant, let me direct you to one of my wedding photos—the toast—for you to understand my ghostly obsession.

My husband and I--using Elaine's ghostly glasses from their haunted gift shop during our wedding toast. Elaine's had its haunted tendrils on me some years ago—even before I knew of the hauntings!

My husband, Carroll, and I happen to be quite the ghostly pair and this was a perfect venue for us. So that evening, in the warm summer hours, we sat eating wonderful food in Elaine's delightful comical theater, with things moving, zipping and zapping around our feet, creepy and fantastically funny actors tickling our bones, and the smell of burning Johnny (he gets electrocuted every night) in the air—it was a perfect way to begin our lives together.

The thing I find curious now, and the question on my mind, is: *Why didn't I see a ghost back then?* I've been told that the more time you spend around real psychics, the more aware you are of the spiritual world. Others have said that some people need a catalyst for the sight to begin. I suppose I wasn't ready for the exploration process at that time—what with romantic thoughts and burning mannequins on the brain. But regardless, I have history with Elaine's, so it was great to be back.

My husband, less dramatic and sentimental, as most men tend to be, saw this excursion as merely a trip to get ghost stories for the book, take some pictures, and get out of the house. Ah, well. Practically speaking, stories *did* have to be collected.

Things were hopping when we dropped by. The Elaine's staff was preparing for a big group in the theater that evening and there just wasn't enough space for the number of people wanting to take advantage of this *trick or treat* extravaganza. (You see, Elaine's is not only incredibly haunted with some very nice ghosts, but it has also been named one of America's top five dinner theatres by The Food Network.)

Ron Long, one of the two owners of this family business, took some time initially to prepare me for some very ghostly experiences by introducing me to one of his employees who was very familiar with the haunted history of Elaine's. Holly Birch, who used to take people on Elaine's ghost tours of Cape May, told us that the building was actually built in 1864, and that the Read family purchased it in 1899. A large family home in plantation style, there have been additions and changes made—particularly when its name was the Winchester, a large tavern inn. (This part of the house was located where the current theater sits.)

The Read family moved to Cape May from Philadelphia. It was a summer home, but as time went on, more and more time was spent in this treasure near the sea. The Reads had one child, Emily; and though it is not known exactly what her illness was, it was debilitating enough for the family to want to be near the clean seashore air. The family spent a great deal of time here.

As the sad story goes, young Emily died in the house, but there is some discrepancy regarding her age at the time of her death. Holly advises that some people say the child died at eighteen years of age, but she didn't think that was true. Other literature indicates the age of death to be thirteen, and she leans towards this theory—or possibly even younger. Holly bases her opinion on the many visitors to

Elaine's who have had current encounters with Emily. Some of those encounters include the staff at the famed establishment. "If you work here long enough," says Holly, "you're bound to meet her in some form, because she's not very shy."

It seems a lot of people have had experiences, and Holly pointed out that some of the things that the ghost does are not indicative of a young woman of eighteen. A girl that age would not have the interest in some of the pranks played.

"What pranks?" I asked. (Inquiring minds want to know…)

Apparently, Emily could be very mischievous in a cute kind of way—covering a room in feathers (more about this later), hiding work tools—silly little annoyances that set most people on edge if they know a ghost is involved. People have also heard her calling for her mother upstairs, and they've heard her crying. Holly tells me, "Ron will be fixing things and find one of his little drills in the ceiling. He'll say that he doesn't know where it is, and then we find it under a ceiling tile."

One of Elaine's bartenders—a gentleman who is not prone to superstitious hearsay of any kind—has changed his way of thinking upon coming to work at Elaine's. He encounters Emily all the time.

Holly believes, too, that there may be other ghosts afoot. "After all," she said, "this is a very old building. We know that she died here. And we are certain that—most of the time—it's Emily. But there were servants who worked here, too; and if there is one ghost, there could very well be more."

I asked Ron, "Why a haunted restaurant theme?" In other words, which came first, ghost or haunted food? He told me they sometimes have murder mysteries, where the audience is invited to solve the crime, but the haunted theme came about because of all the stories they were hearing about the ghost.

Ron said, "The ghost was kind of an urban legend when we first moved in. Right across the street, there is a Catholic school and little kids would tell us that they saw a lady walking up in front of the cupola (located on the second floor at the front of the building). But, you know, you don't pay attention to things like that. I run a dinner theater—I don't pay attention to legends. Then, over the years, so many things would happen that couldn't be rationally explained, and people would see so many odd things..."

And odd certainly begins to describe the goings-on at this inspiring slice-of-life location. They've had people leave during intermission breaks in tears because a real ghost has strolled up to them for a chat!

Most people seem to describe nearly exactly the same ghost—a young lady in Victorian clothing who makes it known that she does *not* like it when anyone makes fun of ghosts.

Throughout the years, Elaine's has been famous for setting themes for its productions and eerie events. During my first visit, a very colorful and creepy joker greeted me at the door.

This is a bit hard to do for the people putting on the productions at Elaine's because, as everyone attending knows, the shows they produce are basically of supernatural or paranormal flavor. These are fun presentations, with lots of laughing and upbeat entertainment.

"The shows are about mummies, ghosts, other dimensions, leprechauns, Atlantis—always some unusual theme. But the themes are only *theatrical* in nature. People like that kind of thing," Ron tells me. "We've had people want to come here to hold a séance or something of that nature, but we don't want to do that. We don't want to open any spiritual doors—or be marked as a place for ghosts to hang out!" (It's true that you never know who will turn up if the invitation is put out there for just *any* ghost!) But theatrical or not, it would seem that sometimes the ghosts feel that the laughs are at their expense.

"We have a really good rapport with our ghosts," he goes on to tell me. "We've had comments over the years from those who are sensitive to the paranormal, and what they tell us is always the same. These people see the same ghost. And the ghost will say to them, 'we don't like it when you are making fun of us.' Over the years, I must have had a dozen comments like this."

Still, it appears to be only a mild reprimand. I believe that the ghost—or ghosts—at Elaine's have too much class to show any severe negativity—from what I've personally heard and seen.

"Our delivery people have seen the ghost," continues Ron, "out of the clear blue sky. In fact, almost everybody who's worked here has seen the ghost—at least once or twice. It's filmy. Some people see orbs. We've had a lot of photographers and psychic researchers who have stayed all night. They've set up cameras everywhere, and they pick up streaks of light and orbs of energy all over the building."

Interestingly enough, my photographer husband took a photo at the bar while I was talking to Ron, and the filmy presence that Ron mentioned appeared in the photo.

During my first visit to Elaine's, my husband Carroll shot this photo of a filmy presence hovering around the bar. At that time, we'd noticed that this section of the bar was much colder than the rest of the room. The photo was taken with a 35 mm camera, and when developed and under magnification, I could see a filmy form that appeared to be a woman's head (with blonde hair pulled up) in the mirror behind the bar. No one in our group had blonde hair. I've attempted to enlarge that portion of the photo here, though it is not as clear as the original. In the close up shot, the phenomenon can be seen in the center of the photo above the bottles.

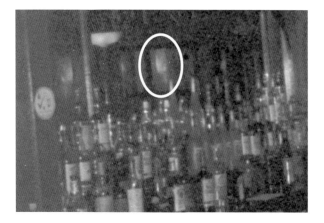

The components of the photo are difficult to see, but I took out a magnifying glass to get a better look. The filmy presence is clear enough, but under magnification, you can see something that looks like the side of a face reflected in the mirror (shown in the middle of the picture)—a light-haired woman with her hair tied up. Yet, there was no one matching that description with us that day. This was very interesting—but just the beginning of a truly haunted expedition to come.

It seems that the ghost at Elaine's is none too shy when it comes to photography. Not only have researchers gotten orb activity, but also the general public is often pulled into ghostly picture taking—and capturing. A gentleman who had taken Elaine's Walking Ghost Tour a few years ago videotaped it, so he could later show it to his family. Once he'd gotten home and had time to view his tape, he called Ron with great excitement.

Apparently, in front of the building, which is where people always report seeing a lady ghost, the man's camera caught the entity on film. A cloud of light came down from the roof and porch area to hang right over the tour guide as she talked about the house and its history. It appeared to be listening as she talked of the ghostly events that had taken place over the years. When she was done telling the story, the ghost floated away—through the wall of the house. The gentleman who caught the ghost on tape was ecstatic! It was proof positive for him that there was a ghost at Elaine's and it was not just a figment of the imagination!

Ron told me that he's seen the ghost many times. "Whenever I see something, I don't see an actual person; I see light. It's usually a spectrum of light—much like looking through a prism; it'll be all the different colors of the rainbow. Generally, though, with this spirit, you don't see it all the time—you feel it."

But the feeling he described is not always a comfortable one. He said he often suffers discomfort, as though he were intruding upon someone's life: "It's as if you've accidentally walked in on a couple kissing, or seen someone dressing. An embarrassment. It's as though I've invaded its space. And it catches you unaware."

I reflected on his description, wondering whether the ghost reciprocated that feeling.

It's been noted through the years that the ghostly activity at Elaine's is most active in the spring and

This shot of the second floor porch shows the location where people on the outside looking at Elaine's front side usually see ghostly activity. It is also the location where the gentleman taking video of the ghost tour saw the cloud of light disappear into the building.

fall. Things do happen in the winter and summer, but the change of season tends to bring about the most activity. This made me wonder about perceptions of levels of activity. The busiest time of year for Elaine's is obviously during the summer when Cape May is packed full with beach-goers and general tourists. Their business has been built on this trade! So if what was happening during my visit was minimal—most definitely winter on this occasion—yikes! What would spring bring?

*But why was this seasonal activity so pronounced?* I wondered. Ron was not entirely sure and speculated that maybe the energy at those times of year was unusual in some manner of speaking. He noted that there was a lot of energy in the air and that people often see shadows.

"Frequently," said Ron, "I've had somebody tap on my shoulder—only there's no one there. And, of course, something everyone says is that they see something out of the corner of their eye. That happens constantly."

Most of us have had experiences of peripheral vision in one form or another. It's an important part of the visual process—a part that happens just outside the center of one's gaze. In many cases, this is the part of vision that averts accidents or identifies some other warning. Though it's weaker in humans (animals have a fairly good sense of this), and while there is a difficulty in identifying colors or shapes, this visual ability has been deemed important enough to be part of the eye exam that a person takes when applying for a drivers license (at least, I've experienced this in those I've applied for in the Mid Atlantic states over the years). It's movement that should not be dismissed nor thought of lightly.

Having said that, what I have found is that, to our ghostly detriment, this is exactly what we do in our human capacities—we doubt our peripheral vision and dismiss it as something not really there. Unless, of course, it keeps us from being involved in an automobile accident—where you most often hear the positives of peripheral vision. (Hmmm, maybe that's why it's on the eye exam...)

On the other side of the peripheral argument, it's also been said that because this kind of vision is super sensitive, when the brain gets tired, the signals can be misinterpreted visually. Personally, though, I feel that if you are in a haunted place and there are multiple reports of people seeing ghosts, relying on your peripheral vision is imperative.

At any rate, take this note from a paranormal investigator (me):

Do not dismiss experiences related to peripheral vision. But do consider what's happening around you during the particular situation in question.

Seeing things out of the corner of the eye is a minor issue at Elaine's though, since there is so much physical phenomena happening there also. "There's such a wide range of things going on here," said Ron. "Tools—and even furniture—will disappear and then later return."

Ron is quick to remind me that the hauntings at Elaine's are not like those where a particular incident is just repeated over and over and over—with no thought or knowledge of the world as we know it. Called a residual haunting, an example of this kind of imprint haunting was told to me while I was researching my book, *Ghosts of Valley Forge and Phoenixville*. People were able to sit in their hot tub on the back of their property and witness revolutionary soldiers coming across the field towards them only to disappear right before reaching the hot tub. This was a reenactment of a historical incident—repeated over and over in time, superimposed on an area like an electromagnetic recording.

The ghosts at Elaine's were different. These entities interacted with those around them—something I was to become privy to later. The incidents here were happening in "real time."

One thing that impresses me is the number of people who come to Elaine's *not* prepared to believe in ghosts, but leave *very much* believing. A family member of Ron's was the perfect example. "My brother-in-law doesn't believe the planet is round!" said Ron, playfully. This was a man who was exceptionally skeptical of things he couldn't see or understand. During a visit to the bed and breakfast, he had stayed on the third floor. (As a side note here, let me say that there is no floor above the third floor.) While there, he couldn't sleep because he kept hearing footsteps and people talking all night long—*on the floor above him*. He knew that no one was - or could be - there, but there was talking and walking and noises—he had heard them. So now he understands and believes.

Ron told me that these "complaints" are not really complaints at all, but rather customers just letting him know about the incidents. "It's not at the level that disturbs people. We've never had anyone actually complain about it—just that they were aware of it. They know there's a ghost walking around."

Ron was very serious about this ghostly interaction. "This ghost interacts; it's an entity. It talks to people... and relates to people... and interacts with people. You hear it... you see it. You hear footsteps. You hear giggling."

These are all of the things that make for a very realistic and interactive haunting—but a nice haunting in the case of Elaine's. Guests have continually told staff that they would hear knocking on their doors and a child giggling in the hallway. But there are no children there. When doors are opened to investigate childish shenanigans, there's no one to see or hear. This has been going on steadily for over seventeen years. The staff has, in fact, grown to expect it—and when the activity slows, they are disappointed because they are so used to it. But not to fear, it always starts up again, and the ghostly balance is maintained.

### Psychic Intervention!

Though my first visit to Elaine's was informative, I knew that I would need to spend more time with Ron and the staff to really get a good feel of what was happening there. But knowing my own inadequacies, I wanted to incorporate an outsider—someone who knew nothing of the establishment but who was ... in touch with the spiritual side of things.

This was when I called Laurie Hull, director of Delaware County Paranormal Research, an informal Pennsylvania ghost research group who maintains that the belief in the paranormal is a personal choice—and for her and her group, it's a rational one, "leaving belief and disbelief behind in order to be objective and open to all possible solutions." Though her website says that those in her group are not psychics, having had my own personal dealings with her, I beg to differ. She's the real thing—despite her desire for a low profile (which I certainly understand). Laurie is also an area representative for the American Ghost Society, chosen to serve the general public and other ghost hunters in the area involving anomalous events and hauntings in the state or region. In other words, much like the directors of the group I belong to (The Chester

County Paranormal Research Society), she knows her stuff.

She is also clairaudient—she hears things. Or at least, that's *my* perception. Laurie has corrected me by saying that she doesn't actually *hear* things; the thoughts or pictures are just in her head somehow.

It was my intention then, to talk with her not only about other area haunts, but to involve her personally in my next interview at Elaine's. She accepted.

It was still off season when the interview was scheduled, but it was the best time to have full access to all of the haunted areas, as well as the undivided attention of Ron Long. Because it was the end of March, the staff was in preparation mode, readying itself and the premises for the onslaught of beach goers who would descend upon them in just a couple months. The heat for the building was not yet turned on and the temperature remained in the high 50s while we were there; low lighting aided us throughout the day. Cleaning was the order of business, with necessary supplies scattered about and materials for sets and scenery out for selection. Stored items were being moved from various rooms and the groundwork was being laid for the interviewing of actors and actresses for the upcoming dinner theater season.

I knew this was going to be a productive day when, out of the blue, Laurie spurted out, "Ghosts don't like obnoxious people!"

I blinked, wondering who in the world she was talking to. Both Ron and I stopped talking. (I suspect that we both were wondering whether she was talking about us!)

Ron took a moment to tell Laurie how many people have told him that the ghost had this very sentiment. He went on to tell us a bit more about the history, adding to what Holly had said on my prior visit. "This place was built 1868 or 1869 by a wealthy guy—the whole story goes back to his daughter; this is where it really all starts. Emily Read. She was an invalid from birth, so Mr. Read built this house for her—and he put a lot of unusual things in to accommodate her. Sunrooms were constructed so that she could go out in the winter or experience the weather because she was wheelchair bound."

Though this looks like a linen closet today, it was an elevator when Emily was alive. Here, Ron Long, owner of Elaine's, uses an EMF meter to detect electromagnetic activity. Though you cannot see the meter flashing red in a black and white photo, the meter is showing activity of 2.5 to 3.0 inside the "closet" (and away from any other normal electrical activity).

"He had one of the first Otis elevators in America installed in the building. The elevator shaft is still here, but long defunct. It was put in before the turn of the century—an ancient thing. Psychics have told us that since the young girl was wheelchair bound, when she passed over, she stayed here because she loved the house and was finally able to roam without any encumbrances."

Further research by Ron's sister-in-law (through exploration at the Cape May Library and Courthouse) reveals that the original property was a huge one, and also supported horses and stables. An old aerial photo indicated to her that, in approximately 1923, there was nothing but trees and little out buildings on the property.

Ron believes that the people who see a ghost at his establishment all see the same ghost. Though they see either a child or a young woman, he personally believes that the ghost is manifesting the same person at varied times of her life.

There is a consensus among some that supports this theory. One belief is that if a person dies young (even as a baby or fetus), that the person then grows up in the spirit world, going through physical stages as someone would in the "real" world. Of course, this speculation, as with many things paranormally related, is up to the interpretation of the believer.

Laurie, who had remained quiet and deep in thought up to this pont, suddenly said, "When we were outside…the third floor seemed to be a center of some kind of activity. I feel that just from being outside—without being on the third floor."

Again, we discussed the local "urban legend" brought to light by the students at the Catholic school across the street, that goes back decades, of the lady looking out the front windows on the upper floor.

Laurie, however, is frowning. "Something is not right..."

But her words trailed off as we ascended to the third floor to begin our "investigation"...

Again, Ron Long, who has become a fellow ghost investigator during this trip, finds high EMF levels in the hallway. Laurie, Ron, and I also felt cold breezes following us throughout the tour.

### An Eavesdropper on the Third Floor

As we ascended the stairs, Ron told us that many paranormal investigators have come and set up equipment, with some leaving it for as long as a week in order to ascertain who—or what—was haunting the establishment. The only equipment that Laurie and I have brought with us this day were two digital cameras (with extra batteries), two tape recorders (with extra batteries), and an EMF meter (see glossary). We explained the usage of the EMF meter, letting him know that he needed to keep apprised of other electrical phenomenas, like air conditioning and light sources, that might influence the meter readings, as well as the range most representative of the electromagnetic energy. He was then assigned to keep track of the readings registering on the meter throughout our tour of the building. (For anyone not having the opportunity to use this kind of meter, it's usually quite astounding when there is actual electromagnetic energy present—and fun. Ron was no exception in finding this ghost gadget exciting. He enjoyed seeing the "hot spots" and found himself even more amazed as the day went on with the amount of activity in his building. Very seldom was the EMF meter quiet—it was nearly always pulsing red light, an indication that energy was abundant.)

Laurie stopped suddenly. "Someone is definitely listening to us," she said, as she gazed around at the third floor surroundings.

It was the attic and not part of the living spaces for those in the past, but used for storage. When Ron became owner, the ceiling was lower and had been knocked out so that height could be added to accommodate the very nice rooms now there. This area was completely shut down for the winter—no water or electric—and that made readings from our EMF more believable.

Our first glimpse of the old elevator shaft, seen clearly from the window, was at this level. Though it did not travel up as far as this floor, the weights and pulleys were still there. "This was the first place to have an elevator in a private home. It used to be right here," Ron said as he opened the closet door and explored the inside with the EMF meter. The area within—now holding towels and such—showed high activity. The EMF readings were highest (about 2.5 on the meter's scale) right in middle of the closet and not near the walls at the elevator shaft. Was a ghost still using the contraption…

## A Well-Dressed Ghost

Moving away from the elevator shaft, the three of us came to a small interior hallway. Here, an old-time Victorian-style dress was exhibited on a bust mannequin. The dress was long and black, nearly touching the floor with an elegance that seemed to be folded into the creases of the dress—even after all these years. It was timeless somehow, and yet very much a part of this new setting.

Ron Long is moving just ahead of me into a hallway where there is a bust mannequin displaying a long black Victorian dress. Laurie feels very strange around the dress.

"There's something about this area of the hallway," said Laurie. (The hair on the back of my neck was standing up for some reason—I never dismiss those kinds of feelings now. They are either *warnings* from beyond or *touches* from beyond. Whether one or the other, in ghost hunting, those feelings say: *Keep your eyes and ears open!*)

"Especially around this dress," Laurie continued, as she turned to Ron and me. "I'm thinking that some of the things going on here are associated with objects—like this dress. When I was outside, I felt that there would be a window here, but now it feels like it's in the hallway where we stand. There's energy. I really think it's that dress."

Ron was quick to respond, telling us the history of the clothing. This was an antique dress—a period piece. Ron's wife, Shirley, who also co-owns Elaine's, used to make dresses upon first buying the property. She would use antique Victorian clothing in the creation of wedding gowns and other special attire. It was her dream to do work for wedding receptions and bridal shops. At one point, she had workers in the building making dresses and wedding things. Of course, who knew that the paranormal world would be so appealing to the masses? It wasn't long before there was not time for her sewing pursuits—she's given it up for the current haunted business.

It was then that Laurie, who had been taking digital photos, called out that her photographs were showing orbs lingering around the dress. I immediately started snapping photos and found the same to be true.

It's no wonder that odd feelings engulf us in the area of the dress—note the orb at the back upper portion of the dress. It is Laurie's belief that the entity here, is bonded to the clothing rather than Elaine's location. Photos were taken within seconds of each other—one shows the orb, the other does not.

So what does this mean? From Laurie's observations, the energy around the dress was connected to the dress and not the rest of the property, as with the other sightings. This, then, may have been a ghost consistent with the Victorian times and who loved this particular dress and could not bear to leave it behind. There are, in the ghost world, situations where spirits become attached, or bound, to an object and will follow that object wherever it goes. The object is an anchor for the ghost for some reason we may never know. This is often reported from the world of antiques dealers.

### Here, Kitty, Kitty

Meandering down to the second floor, we went into the infamous Room 6—the most haunted room at Elaine's.

"This is where I first saw the ghost," said Ron, as he led us inside. "I came up here around eleven one Saturday night, getting ready to go home. There was a little abandoned office up here—"

Ron was cut off in mid sentence as the EMF meter started to flash red, "I'm getting something! Something just passed by me!" He swung the meter around him. "It's all around me!"

Ron was not the only one getting something. Laurie and I both were experiencing strange sensations—air moving, goose flesh, a heavy feeling in the air...

Laurie directed Ron to the door. "Is it around the door? Because I feel something is around the door."

Ron, however, was insistent. "It's in the whole room; the whole room is lighting up—it's charged!"

Laurie and I began snapping pictures. But my camera battery drained and Laurie's was going down as well.

Ron was still by the door, I was in the middle of the room, and Laurie was standing by the window. "You're going to think I'm crazy," said Laurie, "but I'd swear there's a cat here. I keep hearing it and I keep seeing it out of the corner of my eye. I just keep feeling this cat that was so very close to someone."

Ron quickly advised that cats have always been attracted to the building and that they have been known to see ten to fifteen feral felines living in the area at any one time.

However, Laurie did not think this was a feral cat, but rather a pet.

"Someone's pet," she said, still reaching out with her mind. "A cat that sat next to someone once, a cat close to a person."

This was not something that had been reported to Ron before, though he did not dismiss it. It seemed as though the young girl, Emily, loved animals and, in particular, the horses that were raised on the property. It was noted that on horse farms, there are usually barn cats, so this could've easily been a cat

Room 6, the most haunted room at Elaine's, had high EMF activity. Ron recorded the whole room as "hot." For me, this is an especially exciting room, because it's where I saw my first ghost—a cat, scurrying around the door at baseboard level.

attached to the household or to a person who once lived there.

It was then that Laurie reported a loud noise in the hallway—Ron and I did not hear what she was hearing. "This is a loud noise," she said. "Can't you hear it? If I were in this room trying to sleep, it would wake me up. It's that loud!"

Ron and I just looked at each other, a shrug in our eyes.

"Not like a rolling sound—cause I know Emily was in a wheel chair—but like something else. Something going across something…"

"This used to be the servants quarters for the main mansion. This is where the servants lived. Maybe…" Ron began.

"Someone pushing something across something," said Laurie again. "And I think there wasn't carpet in the hallways."

"May have been a cleaning cart," said Ron. "There were always hardwood floors in here—no carpet."

"And it's always cold in here," Laurie added. "… colder than it is now. They're saying that it was always cold. But there's more than one spirit."

The spirits were talking with her now. They were telling her…

"This floor is actually false," Ron said. "Underneath it is the real hallway."

"Is it kind of like a creaky floor?" asked Laurie.

"Oh, definitely. They built that up because the old hall was no longer good. They wanted to make it all one level so they built over the old hallways."

"Maybe that's what I'm hearing."

I had to ask, "Is there more than one ghost?"

Laurie was nodding now.

"There's definitely a cat," she said. "… and then there's this noise in the hallway … it's a constant."

### Cats—that is, Birds of a Feather...

It was now that Ron was compelled to tell a story of Room 6—one of the first stories about it. Guests were staying in the room and their two teenage daughters were staying in the adjoining room. When the teens woke in the morning, they were covered with feathers. Not feathers as those found in a goose-down pillow—long, big feathers. Housekeeping would come

Ron, taking EMF readings, listens carefully as Laurie gets impressions from the room. In this room, the batteries in our equipment are drained. (But that's okay—I saw the cat!)

into the room for a long time after to find piles of feathers—feathers placed in neat little piles.

"Was it from the cat bringing in bird feathers as gifts?" I asked. (Cats are known to provide their owners with little prizes from time to time, showing off their prowess in the feline world. I can still remember my mother screaming at our cat about this "bad" behavior.)

Ron frowned at that, "Could very well be. *We* thought it was an angel sign."

Laurie had been quiet as the story unfolded and Ron and I discussed the meaning of feathers in this particular instance. "Do you want to hear something really bizarre?" she said. "Yesterday, in my house in the living room, I found a pile of purple feathers—I have no idea where they came from. We have a bird, and he's yellow and blue, but these were big feathers.

We have nothing in our house that has purple feathers, nor feathers this big. I just thought it was some odd thing; they just appeared."

Had Laurie been given a sign prior to coming that *someone* knew she would be visiting?

"These were big white feathers," Ron continued.

Laurie seemed to remember that seeing feathers indicated that there was some kind of spirit present and thought that it was possible that the late John Lennon (of Beatles fame) had said that he was going to use white feathers to show his spirit. (Was John Lennon at Elaine's? Sorry…had to ask, being a Beatles fan.)

Ron mentioned that there was much power involved with feathers when considering Indian lore, and Laurie stated that up until the 60s, a feather in your hat was a very big deal, especially ladies with ostrich plumes. They used feathers for pins. This was where the saying, "a feather in your hat" came from, to signify that you had money or *were* somebody.

Through some simple Internet research (Yahoo's *Ask* program), I found this quote about the meaning of feathers:

> It's someone who has passed on leaving you a sign that they are visiting you from the other side. It's just their way of saying, "Hello, I'm here, notice me!" Symbolic meaning: You are loved and remembered by everyone in this life and past lives, too.

Laurie suddenly begins talking again, as she receives impressions from the other side. "The people that were here, they are saying something like... alcohol—there's no alcohol in the house."

"Maybe they don't like the bar," answered Ron. "That's really interesting because this room, before it was changed over, was where they stored their alcohol. They kept wine up here."

"They say there's not supposed to be alcohol. That's all they are saying," Laurie added.

Interestingly enough, when dealing with ghost phenomena, the incidents do not calmly happen one at a time, in a pattern that is easily followed. In the past few moments we had jumped from feelings, to cats, to feathers... And now, back to cats.

*I SAW IT*.

Yes, the cat. I saw the dearly departed dead cat.

Ron and Laurie were talking about alcohol and I actually saw the cat scoot out the door. It was an out of the corner of the eye, peripheral vision kind of thing (and my brain was not tired). *I SAW IT*—my first actual ghost. I'd experienced much over the prior year, but this was the first time I'd actually *seen* a ghost!

I couldn't see more than a whir of quick form, low to the floor, the size of a cat, quick like a cat, grayish in color. *But I SAW IT*! (Who cared about the alcohol discussion at this point? I was practically jumping up and down!)

Laurie, of course, is no longer impressed by the cat. (Been there, done that.) "He's all over the place," she said.

Both Laurie and Ron have hair standing on end now. I don't feel that. But I saw the blur of the cat! Then they were back on the alcohol thread and I had to put the kitty aside for the moment.

"You said no liquor, and this was a liquor storage room," Ron continued.

"Maybe they are just saying that there's not *supposed* to be liquor in this part of the house."

Ron shook his head, not understanding why she would get this particular communication and Laurie just shrugged. "That's what they said—that's what the girl said. 'There is not supposed to be liquor in this house.'" This was a mystery.

Ron added a bit of history. "This room was a disaster. When we cleaned away the old wine, the holders were filled with plaster and dust and dirt. But that was more recent. That's when they first came in here and used it as a restaurant—they used it for a liquor storage area. This was not back when people actually lived here. This was about ten years ago."

"Hey," interrupts Laurie, "I see the cat, too."

(That made me happy.)

We leave the most haunted room of the inn—Room 6. (The room…with the cat—Okay, I'm obsessed with the cat. It was my first.)

### A Touch of Ireland

In the hallway in front of the most haunted room —where cats of days gone past may dwell — the EMF meter was flashing like a giant red beacon. Ron was seeing wavy lines appearing like heat drifting up from hot asphalt, Laurie's feeling heavy air and breezes, and I was feeling cold spots when there was no temperature variation—a smorgasbord of sensation.

The ghosts are following us around, as curious about us as we are about them. Laurie tells us that electromagnetic energy, as it passes through your body, feels like a cold breeze—this is one of the things we were experiencing. We were *feeling* ghosts.

We note, though, that various areas (both in the rooms and in the hall) make the EMF meter glow red at times and then, without ceremony, just stop. Ron made a good point. "I think that it's better that the meter goes off and on in the same location, because then you know that it definitely wasn't something that was in the room causing it naturally."

"The first time I saw the ghost," said Ron, still brandishing the hot EMF meter, "it was light, a spectrum. It came out of that wall where the elevator shaft was and went across the hall and into the wall into this room. [Pointing to Room 6—my cat room.]"

The hallways at Elaine's seem to be especially teeming with ghostly activity. It's as though they walk up and down them quite regularly. In actuality, I believe that they were very curious about us and were following us everyplace we went.

We noted more of our sensations.

> Laurie: "On the front of me, I'm freezing, but the back of me is warm."
> Dinah: "My hand is cold."
> Ron: "[The] side of my face feels cold."

We also noted that the energy was moving all around us. Not only was there the feeling of cold air, but also the EMF meter was continuing to flash red in the 2.5 to 3.0 range—which is in the high probability zone for ghostly energy.

"It might be an energy line," said Laurie.

"A line of force? Feng shui through here?" Ron asked.

We tried to interact with the energy, which now seemed to be close to me (this is at arm's level and not floor level as the prior cat). Laurie asked if the ghost would allow us to take a picture today. We were going to try for orb photos anyway...but it never hurts to ask. A ghost who responds to polite inquiries just may show up on film for you. Stranger things have happened...

This lovely bed and breakfast room was where, at one time, an Irish maid resided—she hated carrying the water upstairs (the servant's stairway was located right outside this room). Laurie and I have speculated that the image in the mirror of the bar area may be this young woman.

In Room 7 now, we find that the EMF readings (still around 2.5 to 3.5) are behind the door—as if someone is peeking around to see what we are doing. To our left is the servants' stairway and the passage they used to go downstairs. It's a fire exit now, but the old staircase is still there.

Laurie was hearing the ghost again. "The people who stayed in this room were not friendly."

"Customers?" asked Ron, not willing to believe that of his clientele.

"Yes," said Laurie. "The people staying here were not friendly. It sounds like an Irish-accented voice saying it. She says, 'The last people that were in here were not friendly.' Maybe they were not nice to each other and that's what she means."

I wondered if this woman might be a servant.

"I think so," said Laurie. "I was trying to get her to tell me what her name was, but she won't say. She says she would get up in the morning and make her bed, go downstairs, and get started. There were two people in the room, but she's the only one in here now. Maybe even more than two people."

Ron confirmed that this was, indeed, the servants' area and that this was possible.

Laurie continued on. "She slept in a bed with another person. It wasn't a very big bed. The thing that she hated most was carrying the water up the stairs."

Heading down towards the other wing of the house, past Room 6 again, Ron told us that he felt incredibly cold all of a sudden and that he had pins and needles as he walked—the EMF was, of course, still showing a constant reading. "I can feel the cold on my face," he said.

This hallway (just past Room 6) marks the place where the Irish Maid would not cross with us. In years past, there was a wall at this location and the ghost advised Laurie that she was not supposed to be in that part of the house.

All three of us felt the air movement going right along with us down the hall. Suddenly, just before we entered the next wing, Laurie stopped. "The servant says that she does not come into this part of the building."

Ron nodded. "In olden times, this part of the house was separated from the other—we would actually be standing outside here. This," he said pointing to the now open hallway, "was an outside wall."

"She doesn't come in here," repeated Laurie.

Ron continued, "You were outside here. But later, when they closed the elevator in, there was no door here. This was a wall. You couldn't go from one area to another."

"She won't come in here with us," said Laurie.

"They were allowed to come over here to serve..." suggested Ron.

"I don't think that was her job. I think this family had more servants—at least from what she is saying."

### Emily and the Nurse

Our next stop was the famous sun porch where the "urban legends" began. This was where people reported seeing a young woman peering out the windows and walking back and forth—from this very veranda.

We all took note of our feelings — as though walking through an invisible curtain — as we moved out onto the porch: Laurie was feeling a tingling

This is the inside of the porch where people from the outside street see ghostly presences. Currently, all the beautiful rocking chairs are stored here, waiting for the new season to begin, but that did not stop our feeling of disorientation as we moved into the area.

sensation and I felt somewhat dizzy and lightheaded. But there were no curtains, no drapes—just wide-open window space looking out over lovely Cape May. Laurie immediately began to pick up something.

Laurie: "This is a different person. This person was very, very happy here.

73

Ron: "This could be Emily that we are seeing right now." [He is talking about the EMF meter lighting up within the room.]

Laurie: "Did they always call her Emily or did they call her Emmy?"

Ron (surprised): "Emmy or sometimes Lizzy."

Laurie: "I hear Emmy. I didn't hear Lizzy. When you said Emily, she said, 'Emmy.' She still likes to come out here."

Laurie continued. "There's a nurse who is out here, dressed in white. Did they have, when she was little, someone who took care of her? Someone who wore … white—she wore… like a uniform? Not a hat, but she's wearing light colors and is walking back and forth with a little girl. The people seeing manifestations might be seeing this nurse. Not like a medical nurse, but a nurse who was with her to take care of her—like a nanny."

"The house was actually willed to the nurse who took care of her. So she ended up owning the house when the Read family left," said Ron.

*Laurie: "That's what I see up here. The woman that people see is not Emily, but this nurse. When I see her with the young girl, she is pretty young, probably—trying to get into context the era, too…It's the way that she's dressed and her hairstyle that makes her appear much older than she is. She's very young, but the way she appears to me with her hair back, she looks much older. She's small; she's not tall;*

she doesn't have a hat on—sometimes she has a covering on for the sun—but she just wears a little thing on the back of her head where her hair is pulled up. She seems to have medium to dark hair—not blonde, but a darker color hair. Long, light-colored clothing on. She wore dark colors sometimes, though. And she had a very nice voice. Emmy is saying that her voice—when she would go to sleep at night—her voice would always put her to sleep."

Ron: "She always took care of her during her whole life—that's why they left her the house."

Laurie: "Emmy was very happy here. If Emmy is still here, then the nurse is still going to be here. That would make sense. If this woman was taking care of her for her whole life, she wouldn't leave her in death. That's why they're both still here. The way I see them is that Emmy is very, very young, like a little girl."

Ron: "She did reach young adulthood in this house, but she was also a child here."

Laurie: "I see her, and she's really little—she's like this [motioning with her hand as tall as a toddler]. Maybe two-years-old; two or three."

Ron: "It'd be interesting to find out if she was born handicapped or—"

Laurie: "—I think she got sick when she was a baby, before she could develop, and it took awhile for them to find out that something was wrong with her. It was very devastating for her parents. Her father tried everything, she said. Took her to all these doctors, all these people trying to figure out how to fix the problem. It was very hard on her father. He never stopped trying to find a remedy, even after she got older. If someone suggested something, he'd want to try it to see if it would work."

Dinah: "Can she tell you what was wrong with her?"

Laurie: "What I'm getting is that she got sick when she was a baby. She's just very weak. And she needed to be carried around a lot when she was little. Even when she was two or three, she was carried around—like out here—and the nurse is here, claiming to have read to her, to brush her hair, and things like that. She seems like she can use her hands, but she gets tired very easily. She spends a lot of time sitting—and she doesn't like to be in bed all day. Cause, she's saying, she's not really sick-sick anymore, she just gets out of breath. I just feel like she gets out of breath when she does too much. The nurse reads to her a lot, so she must've been a very educated woman. Maybe she's pretending to read her stories, though. I think they were very happy here."

Ron: "This was probably a nice place to be, because even in the winter or a rainy day in the summer, you could spend a lot of time here."

Laurie: "In the winter when she would come out here, she would have all these blankets around her. She liked coming out here—Emmy. Even when it was cold. The only time she didn't like being out here was when there was a storm. She didn't like the storms, but even when it was cold in the winter, she would get all bundled up in the blankets. Now did they take her in a horse and carriage thing—they took her places, right? She didn't live just here?"

*Ron: "They didn't live here, this was a vacation home."*

*Laurie: "But she was here in the winter, even later in her life because I do see her. She's not little, but she has all this stuff on [indicating a lot of heavy clothes and blankets]. Did she spend more time here when she got older?"*

*Ron: "I'm pretty sure he had this house built specifically for her."*

*Laurie: "She seems very small, but she may have been older than two or three when I see the nurse with her. Maybe her growth wasn't what a normal child's would be. I can see her walking when she was little, but she got really sick… So she did get to go other places."*

## A Presence in the Bar

We'd been back and forth through the bar throughout the day since this was our staging area. Our supplies and replacements were here, plus the bar was just a comfortable place to be. Though the room was cool, it was also cozy and inviting.

This was the room where my husband caught a ghostly image on film during our prior visit. We talked about this photo and the implications of a fair-haired person (caught in the photo) haunting the room. Laurie reminded us that this was, after all, the servants quarters at one time, and that the woman upstairs whom she'd talked with earlier was fair in complexion and hair.

The bar area was very active with electromagnetic energy. Ron attempts to find areas of natural energy that may be feeding that activity.

Ron advised that around the time of WWI, in the 1900s, the home was no longer a residence. It was used for meetings, and at one time, it was a VFW hall. (Maybe there were ghosts here from multiple time periods?)

We were again taking photos in the room when Laurie announced that not only was there an orb in one of her photos, but that it was a big one. This was in the same location where my filmy white photo was taken.

I, too, photographed several orbs during this current visit to Elaine's.

The entity (or entities) seem to be watching from the doorway and the end of the bar as we talk about our experiences and continue to investigate the bar area. Note the solid orb located at the doorway into the bar at floor level in this photo. The nex photo shows a larger orb.

Laurie and I began snapping pictures quickly and actually were able to show, through photography, the energy moving in the room. We could tell that this was an entity and not just energy. This surprised us because we were under the impression that the bar area was not a particularly "hot" room.

The EMF meter was flashing red at the bar, and as a group, we tried to find what possible electrical receptacles could be nearby that might provide our entity with it's energy. It seemed to be following energy and this energy allowed orbs to develop.

## A Time to Chat

Hoping that we might get lucky and have one of our ghosts actually speak with us on recorder, we set up an area near the bar for an EVP session (see glossary). Putting a chair in the middle of the room near us, but away from any possible energy force, we set the EMF meter down to monitor the energy. It went quiet.

Laurie began the questioning and, following her, we each asked a question, pausing for enough time for an answer, and then continuing with questions around the small circle. In this way, any voices (dead or alive) could be recorded so that later, upon playing the cassette or digital recording back, we'd have the ghost's voice answering our questions. But it wasn't to go that way, I'm afraid.

Here, psychic Laurie Hull and owner Ron Long are looking towards the orb area. Note the chair at the front of the small table. For EVP, we set the EMF meter on this chair (away from the active bar area) where it remained docile through the whole session. (It was our hope that a spirit would come right up to the table with the three of us as we sat asking questions. That did not happen.)

After a few questions and quite a bit of silence, Laurie asked what the people in the establishment now could do to make the spirits of Elaine's happy. She began to get impressions.

*Laurie: "The rooms upstairs definitely need fresh flowers. There's a really strong, clear directive about that. I think there used to be a garden here that had flowers and it's not here anymore."*

*Ron: "This building was completely surrounded by dense woods."*

*Laurie: "When they opened the windows, flowers and the smell of nature came through. It's not here anymore, that fragrance. The scent also comes from some of the plants that were growing outside. And it brought a nice kind of clear calm energy in the house. It kept the people here happier and calm. And they think that the guests here now will be happier, too."*

*Ron: "Even before I'd seen the place, someone I knew recorded a videotape of the property on a walk thru—and you could not see the building for the foliage. Even walking down the sidewalk, it was that dense with vegetation. It's like the house was built in a dense woods—trees thickets, rose bushes, primrose, cedar pine trees."*

*Laurie: "Just a fresh flower scent, I'm smelling right now. [She is thoughtful.] Was that when hydrangeas became real popular? Do you have them here?"*

*Ron: "Yes, and they bloom all summer, too, which is nice. They love the mist that comes off the ocean."*

*Laurie: "I feel like there needs to be a garden or more flowers growing around."*

Laurie asked if there was anything else the spirits might like—and I immediately got the picture of the cat in my mind (of course the cat!). But I've been taught by the Chester County Paranormal Research Society that any thought that pops into someone's head—no matter how silly—should be duly noted during any investigative procedure. This is how the paranormal sometimes communicates. (As a side note, I also think about the feather incident and the fact that Laurie was given a sign prior to coming to Elaine's. This means that someone needs to be cognizant of happenings *prior to* such an investigation/experience/interview—and probably *after* as well. Hmmm, I guess I'm saying that someone should *always* be aware of the signs around them, for they are often indicators of the spirit world and their desire to communicate.)

*Laurie (smiling): "I just heard the cat again [she meows in mimic]. [This confirms my feelings.] Cats are very complex animals. I think they have a strong connection to the spirit. Many cultures fear or worship them. They have some kind of power. Most animal spirits are cats."*

*Laurie, back to the EVP experiment: "Do you like the shows that go on here? [Pause.] They'd like to see more dancing."*

Ron: *"Now that's interesting, because if they were from Ireland or other countries, they'd probably like the singing and the drinking...*

I jump up from my seat. "I saw something again!" (I'm so vocal and excitable when it comes to seeing ghosts, I'm finding.) As Ron and Laurie were talking, I got a split-second glimpse at what appeared to be a black ball at chest level in the doorway that enters into the theater. I'd instantly recoiled, thinking *black* equaled *evil*. Then, immediately, almost as if mentally slapped for jumping to conclusions, I received the words *top hat* in my mind. The ball vanished.

This is the hallway/foyer going into the theater area where I saw the black ball and had the impression of a top hat. The sighting was at Ron's chest level, though he was not in the hallway when I saw the phenomenon—he rushed there right after. This is also where many folks have left the theater to tell the bartender that they'd talked to a ghost.

Yes, it was a black top hat—I know, I know, I said it was a black ball. I can't explain it. I just know that it was a black hat. I was so excited—two sightings in one day. Oh, how I loved Elaine's!

Ron wasn't too surprised. "That's where the ghost comes out to talk to people. I can show you the spot. It's one of the big hot spots where the bartender used to tell me people would see the ghost go into the theater—even though this area is not—"

(Interruption.)

*Laurie: "— It is a man back here. And the one by the door here."*

*I'm speaking into the tape recorder now: "We are right outside the door to the theater, at the door where the servants pass through [when going to the bathroom]."*

*Laurie: "Was there an outside door that came into here?"*

*Ron: [Pointing around a corner to a back entrance.] "Yes, back here."*

*Laurie: "Okay, cause I feel like he's coming in from the outside, and he was scraping his shoes off."*

*Laurie to me: "Was it tall like a man?"*

*Dinah [Wide-eyed] "No, it was round and it was dark—not a man. It was a flash of something…"*

*Laurie to Ron: "Do people here see a man?"*

*Ron: "A woman."*

*Laurie: [Sounding confused.] "Why do I see a man?"*

*Ron: [Speculating] "We could be bringing this guy in because of all the activity. He could be drawn to it…"*

*Laurie [nodding]: "I've parked here before and the parking lot is real creepy at night."*

*Ron: "Yeah, this is a spooky town. More than five or six times we've had people sitting in the theater, and they've seen and heard someone come through this door telling them that they don't like people making fun of the ghosts. And it's almost always people who are sitting right here [where we were standing] looking at spirits coming through that doorway [where I saw the black ball]. This area is much newer than what was here before. In fact, there was nothing here before—just gardens, grounds…"*

Preparations are underway for a new season in the theater—we all wonder how the ghosts will like the new program!

### *"Don't Go In The Basement!"*

How many horror movies have you watched and
said (out loud to the ridiculously stupid heroine or
hero on the screen), "Don't go in the basement!" So
where do we go? That's right.

But not to worry. Well, at least not yet. Elaine's
basement is another world. Fantasy lives down there—
as in most places where actors and other theatrical
people spend their time. There were racks and racks
of fantastically wonderful costumes—oh, how tempted
I was to don a new persona! In fact, the entire basement takes someone out of any *present* and throws them
into an entirely different frame of mind. I could have
spent hours in this basement trying on costumes and
becoming part of Elaine's historic presence.

Also prominently displayed were old posters of
shows long past, comical and spooky reminders for
those rushing to and fro during current productions.
A makeup table was scattered with supplies needed
to turn the everyday person into a haunted mansion
character. A treasure trove of delight!

But it was a basement—and one in a haunted
house. So, as with most basements in haunted surroundings, it was dark and creepy this day we chose
to explore. Oh, there were costumes and fantastic
paraphernalia alright! But there was also gloomy,
low-lighting conditions. And because so many costumes were packed into a tight space, one never

knew when a ghost might slip out from between the racks...

Moving beyond the clothing, back into the substructure of the basement, Ron told us that few places in Cape May actually had basements. Apparently, too (and this does not surprise me), lots of orb photographs have come from the basement from various pieces of camera equipment set up and left in pitch blackness. (I imagine that it might be terrifying in total blackness, costumes falling down around me and on top me...theatrical aren't I?)

Ron confirms this for me when he tells me that he is used to seeing a lot of shadows walking by him as he works alone in the basement. The actors, as well, have found that they sense spiritual activity in these underground spaces—this being the place they frequent during show times. They've told stories of ghosts walking past them and even hearing their voices.

Shadow people or just shadows that are seen out of the corner of the eye (there's that phenomenon again!) are hot topics in the paranormal world with, as usual, the skeptics and the believers. The skeptics—and in my mind, a skeptic is a person who has not had the "opportunity" to see one of these shadows—feels that shadows are merely part of an imaginative person's mind or wishful thinking. Our minds playing tricks. Illusions. Or possibly real shadows caused by another light source (automobile or flash lights, etc.). It's the old *there's an explanation for everything* point of view—which I must say, every ghost hunter I've met goes through the same thinking process to eliminate all the natural sources before considering the supernatural.

Those seeing this phenomena have no doubt that it's real. But it is true that many researchers believe that the shadow people are not the same as ghosts. With those seeing ghosts, usual reports consist of an entity that is filmy white or gray in appearance. Oftentimes, the ghost will have recognizable features or other details that someone can actually describe—possibly a human (or cat!) outline, clothing, or paranormal suggestions in the mind that tell someone *this is a ghost*.

The shadows, on the other hand, are less specific in that fashion. Someone doesn't see features, vapors, or light—just…shadows. But certainly, anyone whose experienced these shadows, knows that they exist. Are they the same entities as ghosts? The vote is still out—I've heard both sides.

I, personally, observed this phenomenon while researching a library haunting in Phoenixville, Pennsylvania (see *Ghosts of Valley Forge and Phoenixville*) and know that they do, indeed, exist. I was privy to witnessing the same phenomenon under two different circumstances. During the first experience, I was investigating an area of the library along with two other team members from the Chester County Paranormal Research Society. We were stationary and quiet, making EVP recordings. At the same time, several infra-red movie cameras were set up to take various area footage of any moving objects (this is how we caught the nationally acclaimed flying book on video at this location).

Suddenly, and though we were there in near darkness, the room became dimmer still and then went back to the normal, low-light gloominess. Immediately, an investigator from the staging area watching the video in real time came out to ask us if we were moving around because they were seeing shadows on the film. We were not. We'd all seen the light dim as though in shadow and then return to normal. Still, at that time, we were not particularly excited by this. We thought about car headlights and the normal things that people think of when shadows slip by, but not much more was thought about it. Until—

During the following few days, the videotapes were actively studied by the team. The firmly outlined shadow was caught on tape moving into the camera frame in a horizontal narrow shadow form at ceiling level, and then back out of the frame, the same way it had gone in. It was very creepy. And very much a blob of black shadow against a very white wall.

At Elaine's, people are seeing this kind of phenomenon a lot. Personally, I do not think that this many folks are all imagining the same thing. Shadows exist at the Haunted Mansion.

But, back to the basement. There is another section of interest encompassing the oldest part of the building, back beyond the costume and actor lounging area. This area has some historic presence to it—it was where the old furnace room used to be, as well as a coal chute. The wall was broken through to add access, but this was a sub-basement showing the old brickwork and timbers from times past.

Ron advised that even when there was a great deal of construction upstairs (when they were putting the bed and breakfast part of the business together), the ghost moved to the lower portions of the building. "And people would see shadows, things moving around the basement." Still, however, thinking that the ghost in the basement might be Emmy, he continued, "But she's not scary. She doesn't scare people, she's just here." (My thought was: *She?*)

Walking behind Ron and through a narrow passageway into the older part of the building, Laurie began to again have tingling sensations and I became lightheaded. We'd come to realize that this was the way each of us perceived spirit energy that was close by. Laurie and I stepped back and forth into and out of the passage to ascertain if there was something about the location—and, we found that, indeed, there was something in the passageway.

>  Laurie: *"It's really strong right here. It's all over my body here—tingly."*
>  Dinah: *"Is this somebody different?"*

*Laurie: "I think it's gotta be the same guy from upstairs. But what is he doing down here?"*

*Dinah: "Did people work down here, Ron?"*

*Ron: "This is our area—we do all our own construction here. We maintain the building so we keep a lot of our tools and paint…"*

*Dinah: "—and this area of the basement wasn't here at all before?"*

*Ron: "No this is brand new—just dirt here before."*

*Laurie: "There is something here."*

*Ron: "…I've been down here at night, and the day, too, where there is no access to the light, and I've seen people walking past me. Shadows walking right around me. I'm down here a lot by myself working, building, and painting, and there's nobody else in the building but me…and I'll see people walk past me."*

Laurie and I discuss the different perceptions we have in this area and upstairs, and Ron assures us that things are pretty benign—except for the occasional patron who needs to be calmed due to seeing ghosts. But, then, that's what started a lot of Elaine's successful business—the rumors, the legends, and ultimately the real ghostly activity. In fact, when the ghost tour first began, they added the restaurant in the front of the building just so people could get something to eat and take a tour. The popularity of the venture has sky-rocketed through the years.

The basement provides a great place for leftover props—this skull was a favorite of mine!

The basement is the actors' haven, providing a full line of costumes, makeup, and ghostly activities.

### The Haunted Mansion Restaurant:
### A Ghostly Chat

The next area of this fine establishment for us to see was the Haunted Mansion Restaurant—this was a place I loved, having been engaged there some years earlier. The oldest part of the building, you could easily see the old woodwork and how things were constructed years ago. Initially, the living room for the Read family, it was a huge room. Ron didn't know whether it had been divided up into several living spaces during the time it served as the Read dwelling; he suspected that it was—and so did Laurie.

During this visit, the room was not set up as a restaurant as you might think, but rather as a prop room so that they might prepare for the upcoming season. Much like the basement finery, this room was filled with wonderful items that would make any horror fan quiver. Everything from mannequins (with attitudes!) to movie trivia items dealing with the old scary features and people (like Alfred Hitchcock and Linda Blair). I could've spent the rest of the afternoon in this room, rummaging, and ahh-ing over magnificent objects of interest.

The room was so fascinating that I'd forgotten, for the moment, about the ghosts we'd come to talk about. And Ron had advised that even though this was where most of the living was, they hardly ever got vibes or ghostly activity in this room.

At this particular juncture, I noticed a lovely prop that would become one of the focal points of my visit. In one corner sat an electric chair, complete with a horrific mannequin (who undoubtedly deserved "the chair").

The Haunted Mansion Restaurant (formally the living room for that long ago family) is where I'd become engaged to my husband some years ago. Today, it was still in prep-mode with a variety of items placed about—a ghostly spring cleaning! This room, though, is a place that has not had not had too much activity.

*Ron: "Oh, that's Johnny; he gets electrocuted every night."*

Ron goes on to show the architectural features of the home, including the old original parquet flooring, doors, and shutters. We look at the small vestibule that up until a few years ago housed a large stairway out front leading up onto the patio. (This was later closed off when they constructed the current main entrance.) This was a beautiful place, and as Ron asked us to think about how lovely it would be in this room with all the doors open, accepting the beautiful sea breeze, our ghostly thoughts left us for the moment. We talked a bit about how the room may have been at one time, when it was residence and not restaurant.

About fifteen minutes later in the same room, I began talking quietly with Laurie, pointing out to her that some years ago, I'd visited the Haunted Restaurant and had been seated in the far corner.

"Oh, over where the electrocuted guy is…" Laurie said.

"Yeah," I replied.

And as we talked, my tape recorder was on and running.

I find it necessary to now take you outside the tour into the future so that you can connect that future to the present for this story. Once an interview is completed, I find it necessary to transcribe the notes from my recorder for the construction of the book I'm writing. You see, though ghost hunters routinely record interviews, it is not usually for securing the same kind of information as an author needs that same recording for. Laurie would be listening to her recording of the day's events for traces of spirit or ghostly phenomena. Though I am certainly interested in that same phenomena, my primary reason for recording interviews is because I have a terrible memory and need the stories repeated for later writing! I needed to record the various tales and happenings of the day because the chances of me forgetting something important were high.

So, as I'm listening to the cassette through my headphones and typing important stories of the day, I reached the point where Laurie and I were talking quietly in the living room.

Recap: Laurie and I are talking about where I sat the last time I was in the living room-turned-restaurant.

*Laurie: "Oh, over where the electrocuted guy is..."*
*Dinah: "Yeah."*
***GHOST VOICE: "JOH-NEE."***

This was definitely a male voice—not Emmy, not the nurse...it was deep in monotone and very male. Ron had said often during the day, that the ghosts at Elaine's interact with the people working, visiting, or performing there. Interaction. This ghost was not only *listening* to what we were saying, but was *adding to* our conversation! Many times during the day, Laurie also noted that *someone was listening to us*, or *they are listening*. Listening is integral to contributing to both the atmosphere and the conversation.

Further, when I had the recording analyzed by Mark Sarro of the Chester County Paranormal Research Society, he verified that this voice was, indeed, within ghost range and out of human range—I had captured a ghost on tape! According to Mark, "A working theory is that EVPs will happen in a lower frequency range. Upon frequency analysis of the EVP we were able to determine that it was in fact in the range of about 250hz."

(To hear this amazing voice, visit http://www.chestercountyprs.com/evp.htm.)

Also, remember, this was in a room that rarely displayed paranormal activity. But photographs taken that day also show very clearly that in the same area where the voice was recorded, orb activity was also present. The ghost was, indeed, tagging along as we toured the facility. The male ghost—and one familiar with the goings-on at Elaine's.

Though the room has not been too ghostly in the past, this was not so today! Not only did we get a ghostly voice on a brand new cassette tape, but an orb shot as well. Unfortunately, because EVPs are identified later when listening to recordings, I did not take a photo of "Johnny," the prop that gets electrocuted every night!

### Summed Up But Not Over!

Through all his experiences, Ron was able to sum up his feelings about the hauntings at Elaine's:

> *"This is a pretty famous ghost—active and very well documented. A lot of people have acknowledged it over the years. It's a ghost that is interactive—this is an entity that talks to people and interacts with people and relates to people. It's not just watching a sunset and disappearing without noticing things around it. People come here often, and if they are sensitive, then they can sense the ghost. The ghost has been here 140 years and has been reported by hundreds and hundreds of people over that period of time. You could go to twenty places in this town and they would tell you they have a ghost, but this ghost has been seen and photographed by a lot of people."*

I agree with everything he said.

Thus, our paranormal trip to the lovely Elaine's Haunted Mansion Restaurant, Victorian Inn Bed and Breakfast, Dinner Theater, and Walking Ghost Tour ended. But is it the end of the ghostly activity? No—I can safely say, definitely not. In fact, don't take my word for it. I'm sure that you might want to check out their ghostly phenomena for yourself. The gang's all there!

Laurie, staring out of Room 6, recalls through psychic ability, a dreamy past filled with children and nurses and cats and flowers….Elaine's is a warm haunting. It welcomes you.

# Chapter Two
# The Southern Mansion

720 Washington Street
Cape May, NJ 08204
1-609-884-7171 or 1-800-381-3888
http://www.southernmansion.com

---

Directions: Take the Garden State Parkway into Cape May. The Parkway turns into Lafayette Street. Go to the first traffic light and turn left onto Madison Street. Go one block to the first traffic light and turn right onto Washington Street. Southern Mansion is three blocks on the left hand side of the street.

---

## ...Could it be...

She stood on the lushly carpeted stairway looking down onto the foyer leading to where her guests celebrated her marriage to her childhood sweetheart. A feeling of bliss was in the air—here she was in this grandeur setting about to move into a new chapter of life.

Ghostly Aspects:

- *Eerie feelings in lower meeting room*
- *Strong smell of perfume or roses*
- *Breaking wine glasses*
- *Exploding kitchen batter*
- *Physical touches and sensed presences*
- *Cold spots*
- *Door locking itself*

The long silky train of her wedding gown flowed down the staircase offering an image that could stand the test of time. It was a lovely day and it had been a beautiful garden wedding—the first day of pure harmony in her life. It was time now to mingle with her guests and to prepare for the special toast that the best man, her new husband's brother, had prepared for this special day.

She moved quietly down the stairs, with just the rustle of satin in her ears and a light heart filled with a forever kind of love.

The strong smell of perfume startled her. It was a scent that she did not recognize. She looked around. No one was near, yet the perfume was almost overpowering. And there was something else. Not only was there the interesting fragrance, but she felt a presence—a warm presence to be sure, but a real female presence. Only no one was there with her. She stood alone on the staircase. The bride frowned. What was this? A ghost?

She hurried as much as she could, gathering yards and yards of satin into her arms, down the stairs and out into the gardens—wanting to look back, but afraid to. Once she was with her wedding party, she felt silly at having imagined someone there on the stairs with her. No one was there. There was no perfume but her own—mild with a touch of cinnamon scent.

Her husband, also frowning, leaned down to whisper in her ear, "What's with the roses?"

The bride shook her head, not understanding. "What roses?"

"All I can smell is roses and I don't *see* roses, and you're not *wearing* roses!"

The best man interrupted before the conversation could go further, "Are we ready for the toast?"

The newlywed couple nodded, both smiling now, forgetting their varied scent issues.

The waitresses and waiters serving the wedding party were delivering small glasses of champagne, moving in and out of the laughing mingling guests. The atmosphere was happy and jovial.

The best man tapped his glass with a spoon making a tingling sound. The guests turned to the bridal table set in Southern Mansion splendor. He held his glass high to begin the toast. The bride and groom followed suit.

It was then that the glasses of the bride, groom, and best man exploded in their hands.

### Farfetched? The Early Southern Mansion

Built sometime around 1860, this lovely home, turned boarding house, turned hotel, is the largest and most magnificent mansion in Cape May. This beautiful establishment was constructed by George Allen, an industrialist from Philadelphia. He and his descendants utilized the property until the mid-1940s when the last of the family passed on to the world beyond. It was then that the mansion was sold and turned into a boarding house, now lodging those other than affluent Philadelphians. Converting the mansion proved to be problematic, however, and the building became structurally unsafe. Little by little, the house and grounds fell to disrepair and by the 1980s, the property was doomed to ruin.

In 1994, a new Philadelphia family came under the mansion's spell. The Bray/Wildes could not understand why such a lovely home site had been left to ruin. They purchased the house, keeping priceless and important furnishings, artwork, and other valued items—and tossed the rest. The mansion was to be restored!

Reopened as a hotel, a south wing was added to the home, housing additional guest suites, bathroom accommodations, a second ballroom, a kitchen, balconies, a gallery, verandah, solarium, and two beautiful circular staircases. The original flavor and style of the first house was upheld and, by 1997, the house was again ready for guests. The Southern Mansion (named after Samuel Sloan's drawing of the property completed in 1852) was not only restored, but reborn.

But what does all this history of a beautiful mansion have to do with ghosts? In the case of Southern Mansion, history plays a big part.

### The Halls Tell A Story

Owner Barbara Wilde told author Tina Skinner that she believed George Allen's long-haired niece, Esther Mercur, who died of alcoholism, still roams the halls of the Southern Mansion. There have been many who have said that they feel something while at the mansion—nothing sinister; in fact, the feelings relating to this haunting are never harmful or scary. This is something that is especially felt in the lower meeting room—a newer area that welcomes conferences and people from all walks of life. Others have mentioned the smell of strong perfume and roses.

Barbara smiled as she told Tina, "We never have a wedding but that glasses blow up—on a tray or in your hand!" (Maybe this was Esther's interesting way of celebrating a union!)

It would seem that Esther also has quite a sense of humor, though the kitchen staff may not think so. One day, the chef was stirring some batter when suddenly bubbles of different colors—purple and green—came up from the mixture. In fact, they blew up—all over the ceiling! (Barbara advised that they do not have food coloring in the house.)

The ghost at the Southern Mansion gives the impression that she wants to let people know she's around. "It's just like she's saying, 'Look at me,'" said Barbara. "I lived here during the whole renovation and nothing ever bothered me. I'd *feel* it, but it wasn't scary."

Ghost investigators from the South Jersey Ghost Research group also investigated the Southern Mansion in 2004. (The photos—very interesting!—can be seen at www. southjerseyghostresearch.org.) During their stay, members of the team felt the physical touches of ghosts as well as sensing their presence. Cold spots were noted in several rooms and they had an incident where a door locked itself after it had previously been found unlocked.

The Mansion has made it to the covers of *Victorian Homes*, *Agenda Philadelphia*, and *Atlantic City* magazines, so it appears that Esther is on her way! Still, questions remain. Why does Esther make herself known at weddings by bursting glasses? What has her at unrest? Or is this a strange way to celebrate, like those who throw glassware into fireplaces after emptying them of their swirling contents?

As much as researchers would hope that hauntings follow the natural paths of investigation, this doesn't always happen. Though Esther is of prime interest at the Mansion, Ghost Investigator and Psychic Medium Craig McManus has found another ghostly entity with more interest in breaking wine glasses than Esther. If you will recall, before the Mansion was restored, it was a boarding house. During that time, tragedies of various kinds plagued the previous owners—The Crillys. During Craig's investigation, he did not feel that Esther was breaking wine glasses. Rather, Daniel Crilly, turning to bottled spirits as a way of dealing with a neurological disorder, smashed all the wine bottles he'd found in the home—reason unknown. Could it be Daniel who is causing such a ruckus? Could he be angry at wedding guests who raise glasses of spirits to toast? Craig believes that *yes*, Daniel has issues with drinking guests.

Regardless, it appears that Esther and Daniel may be there to greet you when you visit this lovely Victorian treasured manor.

# Chapter Three
# Windward House
# Bed and Breakfast Inn

24 Jackson Street
Cape May, NJ  08204
(609) 884-3368
http://www.windwardhouseinn.com/

---

Directions: Take the Garden State Parkway to the southern end of Cape May, where it becomes Lafayette Street, which dead ends at Jackson Street. Turn left, drive through the Mall and Windward House is about ½ block further on the right.

---

## Ghostly Aspects:

- *Third floor ghost*
- *The Wicker Room and the Irish maid ghost*
- *Orb photos*
- *Footsteps*
- *Banging Noises*
- *Doors locking mysteriously*

*...Could it be...*

"I won't leave!" she said out loud, as she pushed a bureau against the door frame. "I won't be treated like this."

She'd had enough. Yes, it was true that her lover had built her a beautiful home next door to his own home. And the quaint heart shapes built into the shutters had pleased her at first. They were a sign to her that he loved her. It had been enough at first. But why was she forced to share him with that other woman and family? Why wasn't she the one to be in the main house instead of hiding out as his mistress behind the doors of a wanton place? Why shouldn't she be the woman of his life?

Well, she was here now, the gold fabric of her dress glittering in the warm moonlight from the window. In the main house. In the small room on the third floor. Barricaded here so that no one—not even her lover—could remove her.

Catherine may not have been allowed in this house before, but she swore that even after death, she would have access to it. She would not be put out.

## The Story of Wicker

And so the Windward House hauntings may—or may not—have started. No one knows for sure. But owner Sandy Miller told author Tina Skinner that there have long been stories about a ghost that lives on the third floor as well as other tales about this lovely structure. Accounts have mentioned the famous Wicker Room on the third floor and it's ghostly Irish maid. (Could it be she and not the mistress who haunts the Windward or are both walking the floors at night?) Orb photos have been taken by paranormal investigative groups throughout the house, including the servants' staircase. People have heard footsteps and banging noises late in the night.

This exquisite Edwardian-style bed and breakfast inn, located on Jackson Street, the oldest street in Cape May, was built as a private home in 1905, where the family lived until the 1940s. It was then opened as guest cottages. In 1977, it was purchased by Owen and Sandy Miller and opened as the Windward House. Through many restoration projects, it has remained a warm and traditional place of comfort for more than twenty-five years.

In addition to a first floor wraparound porch decorated in wicker, there is a second floor private porch and a third floor sundeck—what ghost wouldn't try to lock itself in this cozy place?

"I don't discount anything," Sandy said. "At this stage in life, I think anything is possible."

As far as her own encounters, Sandy said she did have two events that she couldn't explain scientifically. She'd received a call one day that the powder room off the lobby was locked from the inside. The hook and eye lock was latched from the inside and the staff feared that a guest might be unconscious inside. Desperate to assure the guests' safety, the owners broke through the outside window—only to discover an empty room. Two weeks later, when it happened yet again, they simply pulled the door open, breaking the lock and replacing it with a better one.

"It might have been that the action of slamming the door could make the hook swing up and catch in the lock," Sandy said. But she doubts it because the hook was attached to the jamb, not the door itself. Could this be a lonely mistress looking to finally stay in the main house where she felt she belonged in a lifetime long past? Is she attempting to assert her legitimacy in the afterlife?

### Bathroom Fears

Laurie Hull, researcher and director of Delaware County Paranormal, stays at the Windward House frequently. In the summer of 2006, something that she felt was strange happened to her there.

In her own words:

> "At the Windward, I was always terrified—and this is so silly—to use the bathroom on the first floor. Without knowing anything about this powder room, I was terrified. When we visited this summer, we were happy that the Windward had something available for us on the third floor. But when I needed to use the restroom while downstairs, I looked at that powder room and I thought, 'Nope, I'll walk all the way up to the third floor to go to the bathroom in my room, because I will not go in that bathroom.'

*Then, I picked up Craig's book [The Ghosts of Cape May by Craig McManus] and read that the door in the powder room gets locked from the inside—when no one is inside to lock it! Well, no wonder I didn't want to go in there—there's somebody already in there!"*

But Laurie advises that the room was not always a powder room. She believes that it was part of a closet or pantry where things were stored—things that the owners at the time did not want touched. Therefore, they did not want casual visitors (guests) going in the room.

Laurie said that she feels that the ghosts on the first floor are those of a man and woman, seemingly from different times, but both caring a lot about the house. The man appeared to be from the twentieth century—a more recent haunt; and the woman was much older. When the woman was a real-life resident, things about the house had been different. This powder room area was where she kept things, and she didn't want people going in there. So...she locked the door.

Laurie attempted to tell *her* that the room was now a bathroom and no longer a place of storage. "If," she reasoned with the female ghost, "you lock the door from the inside when there is no one inside, people can't get in to use the bathroom and then get back out quickly." There's hope now that, since Laurie's talk with the ghost, she won't lock the door now. "But," said Laurie, "sometimes a ghost won't entirely believe you. They want to wait and see what happens. They watch."

Only time will tell…

## The Case for Carpet

The third floor ghost is more active. This, too, is Laurie's personal account of a recent experience at the Windward.

> *"In my third floor room, I was suddenly awakened in the night by my fiancée talking. He never talks in his sleep. We've been together for years, and he's never talked in his sleep—never, not once. We travel a lot, and through all the haunted places we've been, he's never talked in his sleep.*
>
> *"But now he's talking. And I cannot understand a word he is saying—the language was one I couldn't understand. I was facing him. The way the room is set up, everything is carpeted, except the bathroom. Now I hear somebody walk on the floor [she makes sounds like clicking heels on wood]—even though it's carpeted. Yes, footsteps on a wooden floor with shoes. The footsteps come into the bathroom, and I'm thinking: Oh my God, did I forget to lock the door? So I jumped up and ran into the bathroom. There's no one there, and I looked out into the hallway and noted that the floors were all carpeted. I'd heard the door open and close, and someone came in. But there was nobody there. It was weird, weird, weird!"*

Laurie's first impression was that someone outside in the hallway thought that this particular bathroom was a community bath because of its proximity to the deck at the end of the hall—there for everyone to enjoy. This was her thinking until she went to the door and found the entrance to the outside hallway locked (and carpeted). "Whatever I heard in the hallway," she remarked, "was not *this* hallway."

Other than her own experiences, Laurie also described to me the happy and contented ghost that most people experience at the House. The haunted room is called the Wicker Room and is located on the third floor. Though the ghost has been sensed by many people, she tells me that only one person has reported actually seeing it; and that woman was staying in the Wicker Room at the time. She opened the door and saw a hazy image of a young woman sitting on the edge of the bed.

The South Jersey Ghost Research team has also investigated this bed and breakfast and have found that most guests encounter an Irish maid in the Wicker Room and in the areas surrounding it. They've gotten as many as twenty-three photos showing orbs at the Windward. (See the photos at: www.southjerseyghostresearch.org/cases/winward1.html.)

This is a favorite place for Laurie Hull, despite the night visitors; and she said that the owners (Sandy and Owen Miller) are amazing people.

# Chapter Four

# The Queen Victoria®
# Bed & Breakfast Inn

102 Ocean Street
Cape May, New Jersey  08204
(609) 884-8702
http://www.queenVictoria.com

---

Directions: Take the Garden State Parkway South to the end when it turns into Lafayette Street—stay in the right-hand lane. Turn left onto Ocean Street and proceed through the light at Washington Street. The third intersection on the right is Columbia Avenue and the Queen Victoria is on the right hand side.

---

Ghostly Aspects:

- *A ghostly woman on the third floor*
- *Eerie feelings reported by guests*
- *Room disrupted or rearranged when the owners were away*
- *Electrical Issues*
- *Exploding Toilet*
- *Smell of Perfume*
- *Bumping movements (against bed)*

*…Could it be…*

The noise was louder than usual this warm May evening—and that was not good. Her very livelihood depended upon her ability to sound the alarm above the sounds of laughing (and groaning) men, boisterous fighting, and shrill women. Her only weapon was the rocking chair and the creaking boards she rocked upon. The fact was that her time in the rooms with the men — and their ever-demanding fantasies — was over. She was past her prime and would be put out of her home if she did not prove useful.

Not that being outside the action instead of inside the rooms was something she missed. It wasn't. She remembered days and years past as she watched the rocker ladies sitting stoically in the chair with such an important job. It hadn't entered her mind that the woman would be wondering how long it would be before she was put out with nothing.

But here she was. It was her job to keep her eyes and ears alert for the law, to warn those in the rooms—the ones who were both gambling and fulfilling their desires on the third floor—when the law was near. The boards were left in disrepair to creak and crackle as she rocked. Most of the time, she sat still in that chair, working with the cloth in her lap. But she did not work on the cloth really. She fumbled with it and moved it here and there, making it appear that she was sewing. No one could tell as she sat on the wraparound porch in her rocker. They did not notice that she did not rock and did not sew. No one noticed her now—well past forty in her age...

### More Than One Place to Haunt

The Queen Victoria Bed and Breakfast Inn is made up of four wonderfully restored Victorian buildings: House of Royals (formerly, and most notable in the ghost world researched here, The Queen's Hotel), The Queen Victoria, Prince Albert Hall, and the Queen's Cottage. Comprised of twenty-one rooms in the heart of the historic district, these remarkable buildings are among the finest.

Purchasing the inn from founders Dane and Joan Wells in 2004, new owners, Doug and Anna Marie McMain, do their very best to captivate guests with hospitality and comfort in their inn, and they succeed marvelously.

Two of the stately buildings built in the 1880s have been restored to their prior magnificence and have managed to keep a specter or two in the process.

In the season of 2004, author Tina Skinner retold the long-standing story of a woman who descended from the third floor late at night and walked toward the front desk. Further, it seems that, though the owners and managers could not say that they'd experienced this ghost, stories still circulate about it. In fact, the inn remains a noted presence on the local ghost tour circuit and they do tell guests about it as a matter of disclosure.

The owners have disclosed that there were various "problems" during renovations, but, not being present, they were not sure of the causes.

Tina was also told by an employee of over twenty years that the previous owners had a room on the third floor where every guest mentioned that they felt *something*. There were stories about the room being disrupted or rearranged while the owners were away.

Laurie Hull had much to say about The Queen's Hotel. The picture she painted was crisp: "This beautiful hotel used to be a speakeasy—back in the day—and the story told is that there was a person who would rock a warning, hard and fast, to let those inside know that the law was coming."

Hull noted that the second floor is said to have been a gambling casino and that the third floor was made available to willing customers as an entertainment establishment of a "more intimate nature." A natural sight would have been of a woman sitting in a rocker on the porch sewing. At the first sign of police, she would rock forcefully, creaking the floorboards and sounding the alert that it was time to hide any discriminating evidence of their illegal activities.

Noted ghost researcher, Craig McMannus, made a debunking statement that made sense regarding this rocking woman. He wondered how anyone inside the establishment embarking in gambling and other goings on could hear the warnings of a porch rocker over all the noise!

Regardless, sensitive Laurie Hull advised that she felt that one of the prostitutes was haunting the building. "Every time I've visited the hotel, I've taken pictures of it. I always get orbs on the second level. I think its haunted."

Personally, Laurie has not seen an actual apparition, but she is always drawn to the hotel on her visits. And each time, she is compelled to stand outside and look up to take her photographs.

Other people, as well, have said that they've seen things at The Queen's Hotel. It's been said that guests have found things moved around in a ransack fashion; room decorations scattered over the furniture and floor in one of the third floor rooms. It was also reported that a toilet exploded for no apparent reason and that the electricity has been known to go out completely on the third floor—also with no cause discovered. The smell of strong perfume and the physical sensation of someone bumping against a guest's bed in the night as if someone were wandering around in the dark, has also been noted.

Though the third floor seems to have a romantic allure, Laurie had the feeling that the second floor held the presence of a woman of the night. " I don't know why I feel that the ghost was a prostitute—I just do. And I always go back and wait for her to come out; but she always stays inside. I constantly get orbs in my photographs—but they appear on the second floor balcony. She's there, I know she's there."

So, whether you're at the Queen Victoria to experience the historic district, the Atlantic Ocean (just one block away) or to rock in one of the fifty "warning" rockers on the porches, this is a fantastic place to be!

# Chapter Five
# The Inn at 22 Jackson Street

22 Jackson Street
Cape May, New Jersey 08204
(609) 884-2226
http://www.innat22jackson.com/

---

Directions: Garden State Parkway South to Cape May. Cross the Cape May Bridge (you will be on Lafayette Street). Follow Lafayette Street to the end and make a left onto Jackson Street. Cross the Washington Street Mall and the Inn is a half block on the right hand side of the road.

---

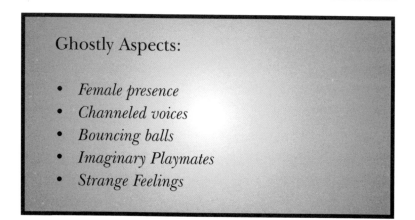

Ghostly Aspects:

- *Female presence*
- *Channeled voices*
- *Bouncing balls*
- *Imaginary Playmates*
- *Strange Feelings*

*...Could it be...*

"That's my ball," said the little girl, pulling it from her brother's hands. Angry, she threw it down the stairs, watching triumphantly as it bounced, bounced, bounced down to the hallway below. "Whatcha do that for?" grumbled the boy. "You know we're not supposed to play with it in the house."

The girl just shrugged. "It won't be *you* that gets into trouble. You know that."

"Yeah, I know, but it's not fair to *her*. And I like her. It's *you* that's a nasty girl." He stomped back to his room to sulk.

At the bottom of the stairs, a young woman stood, the ball in her hands. She was shaking her head in quiet and loving reprimand. "You two know better," she said softly, as she reached out her arms to offer the ball up the stairs.

"Oh, Esmerelda," said the girl. "You know how my brother is. But forget him; will you play with me?"

"Of course," said the woman and she gave the ball a push towards the girl.

The ball floated back up the steps unaided—and Esmerelda disappeared.

### The Jackson Street Crowd

During my first fact-finding visit to Cape May, my husband and I strolled down Jackson Street on the way to the beautiful Inn at 22 Jackson Street, appreciating the architecture and just generally piecing together the stories of so many haunted bed and breakfast establishments within such a short distance. It would seem that it may have been easier to tackle a book about the places that are *not* haunted in Cape May—for the town was filled to the brim with spiritual energy!

Jackson Street holds a haunted appeal to be sure—a strange and fascinating charm that is perfect for delving into history and urban legend. Why urban legend? I'll get to that.

But first, let me say that the feelings we experienced while walking along Jackson Street were especially strange—more so than through other areas (even those that were reportedly haunted). On Jackson Street, one can be strolling along as we were, totally alone on the sidewalks, and yet not alone. But it was more than not being alone. There was the sense of a crowd looming right behind us—nearly in our personal space. It's the uncomfortable feeling one gets when someone is shouting as they stand too close to your face; you want to step back so that the energy is dispersed to an area larger than your own sacred breathing space. Somehow, as we walked, we could swear that there were one hundred people walking behind us—a network, but not of the telephone variety. For you see, when you turn around to see who is following you, no one is. Jackson Street is humming with spirit energy.

An interesting story that comes from the archives (2000) at the website www.capemay.com tells of a young woman living in the area named Nancy (fictitious name). One September, Nancy was working an early shift at an area restaurant in Cape May. Leaving her home in plenty of time to get to her job, she strolled along (where else?) Jackson Street. But it was too quiet that morning—not the usual dawning of day where birds chirped their sweet songs. No air movement, either—despite the fact that by the bay, there was always a breeze of some magnitude. She continued on, though she felt uncomfortable and the hair on her arms was standing on end. (Warning! Remember to note all sensations and surroundings.) Though a skeptic as far as ghosts go, she cannot deny what happened next.

She saw a woman walking toward her, not appropriately dressed for the day. In an instant, she was gone. Nancy thought that she might still be in the area—behind a building or some other place that she was not seeing. But no. In fact, she describes it as "time standing still." And it was then that she heard a young woman's voice calling, "Audrey," its syllables long and drawn out. The calling continued.

Suddenly, the woman appeared again—this time in the middle of Jackson Street. From the interview:

*"As Nancy watched, the figure turned as if looking for something…to Nancy's amazement, the entire figure*

*seemed to whirl around and around. That's when she re-alized that the woman's features were indistinguishable. Her clothes were unclear as well. To Nancy, she seemed just a form; and as she watched, the figure seemed to float an inch or two above the pavement. Toward her..."*

This, of course, was enough to scare Nancy, but before she could think more about the cold chill that was running through her body, the woman vanished. And the day returned to its normal beautiful Cape May day. Thus are the spirits that walk along Jackson Street.

On this day, my goal was to snap a few photos of the lovely Inn at 22 Jackson Street. It stood out along that crowded street—three stories of blue and purple with small twinkling lights adding charm to the verandas and tall turret.

I had already spoken to author Tina Skinner who had interviewed previous owner, Maria McFadden, about the strange occurrences there. Maria advised that when she first came on board, the then-property owners told her that there was a ghost and that she would certainly meet her. And that seems to be true; several times Maria would be in the kitchen when she experienced sudden feelings that someone was walking right by her. She told Tina that her name was Esmerelda and that she was a nanny there many years ago, staying in the turret room on the third floor.

I'd also talked with psychic Laurie Hull at length about the haunted stories that came from this charismatic property. It seemed that everyone knew about the famed Esmerelda and her ghostly reign over the Inn. Apparently, a man came to the door of the Inn one day to ask those living there if the place was still haunted by a wonderful nanny named Esmerelda who tragically died there. Her loving spirit was known to move about on the third floor of the building. Unfortunately, someone was staying in the third floor suites at the time Laurie attempted to get to the bottom of the tale, but that didn't keep her from talking with those who were in the know or going on the local tours to hear the gossip and legend surrounding Esmerelda.

Laurie felt pretty quickly that the story was legend, that the beloved Esmerelda did not exist. Now that's not to say that the Inn at 22 Jackson isn't haunted—because it is. But maybe not in the fashion that the stories have brought forth. In fact, she advised that she's not been able to find documentation for who the supposed gentleman was who came to the door or in what capacity he was there.

"I didn't get a feeling that the presence at the Inn was an Esmerelda...I've only been on the inside, in the front of the building on the bottom—someone was staying there both times I went in, the rooms are always booked. But it was on the ghost tour. And I felt like you could see a person in those windows sometimes [top right windows]. And I felt like the whole third floor was active. I didn't feel Esmerelda as a name, but I definitely felt like a female presence was there. As far as the Esmerelda reports, that name doesn't click."

Her research (from talking with others in the psychic world and those who've experienced the phenomena) brings her to the conclusion that though a female presence inhabits the Inn, her name is not Esmerelda.

This ghost, however, does not make the same impact on her personally as Elaine's ghost. She felt that if there were people present in the room, i.e. staying the night, visiting, or investigating, the entity would retreat from the confrontation. This was why she'd not pushed to stay there for the night to do applied research. Though a gorgeous place (and she notes that "the turret area is very strange, too"), there were other ghosts in other Cape May locations who were much more inviting of her presence and interaction on their ghostly turf.

She, like me, felt much more of an attraction to the actual street outside the Inn. "The whole street, even if you are by yourself, you always feel like other people are there. It's not like other places in Cape May. If I'm down at the beach and I'm by myself, I'm by myself. On Jackson Street, you feel like there are other people there. When you turn the corner, you feel like someone will be there."

She's talked to those historians who've told her that the whole area burned down and, sadly but often true in fires of this magnitude, a lot of people died. My own research confirmed that many hotels were burned due to their wooden construction in the late 1800s. Rebuilding brought back much of the charm of the area, and (thankfully) gave some old ghosts a place to reside in a new world. Laurie feels very certain that there are spirits still walking around the streets of Cape May.

Psychic Medium Craig McMannus has had personal experiences with the ghostly activity at the Inn (see his creepy book, *The Ghosts of Cape May*) by channeling some of the residing (and visiting) ghosts. He also witnessed a bouncing ball ascending the stairs with no person about to do the bouncing! Feeling that the name Esmerelda was not the name of the female presence there, he conducted extensive research and eventually confirmed that fact with the previous owners. Rather the name *Anne* was psychically felt. In fact, the name Esmerelda, according to his discussion with previous owner Barbara Masemore, indicates that the dear Esmerelda was made up. It turns out that the owners in the 50s (the Wolfes) had children who had an imaginary playmate. Name? Yup, Esmerelda. (See Craig's book for the full details.)

So take some time during your trip to Cape May to stop by this very lovely inn—get into the spirit of things! The Inn at 22 Jackson was the winner of the Arrington Bed and Breakfast award for best location in both 2001 and 2002.

# Chapter Six
# Congress Hall

251 Beach Avenue
Cape May, New Jersey  08204
(888) 944-1816 or (609) 884-8421
http://www.congresshall.com

---

Directions: Take Garden State Parkway South (it turns into 109 South). Follow 109 over the Cape May Bridge. The road becomes Lafayette Street. Follow Lafayette through two traffic lights to the end. Turn left onto Jackson Street and an immediate right onto Mansion Street. Go to stop sign and turn left onto Perry Street. Make first right onto Congress Place and turn left into the hotel reception area.

---

Ghostly Aspects:

- *Voices*
- *Footsteps*
- *Shadows figures*
- *Movement (peripheral)*
- *Touches*
- *EVPs*
- *Residual perceptions*
- *Heavy air*
- *Moving objects*

## ...*Could it be...*

He watched the fire burn, but still he could not take his eyes from the leaping flames by the ocean. How could a fire be beautiful when it was so destructive? People were running about, gathering what valuables they could, screaming their fears. But he just stood. Water so close, but not close enough to save the devastation.

Finally, he turned and walked back into the water, for there he would find his home. The sea. The ship. He had his own destruction to face—the *Juno*.

### A Ship's Anchor—and Wreck

At first sight, Congress Hall looks as magnificent as its name. A cool windy morning with sunshine touching the light yellow L-shaped, four-story building with impressive white columns was a welcoming sight for my husband and me. This was definitely a place where the manicured grounds became part of a historical backdrop.

Nearing the building, we were first struck by the immense anchor situated in a garden area in front of the Hall. The plaque in front of it read:

> *Captain John Davies of the 28-ton fishing boat, Fred H. Snow, hooked a 100-pound anchor, June 20, 1968, 12 ½ miles off of Cape May. Careful study of the mold and other factors have identified it as belonging to the Spanish Man of War Juno last sited in 1802, October 27 in a NE storm 25 miles south east of Cape May. Juno was never seen again. There were 425 people aboard and carried $400,000 worth of silver in her hold, plus Mexican treasures of jewels and gold trinkets. She was on her way from Van Cruz, Mexico to Spain. Charles the Fourth was the King; Napoleon had just come to power in 1770. This loss of great treasure might have affected decisions in Europe on behalf of the New World. The anchor was purchased by Dr. Carl Macintyre and placed here on August 3, 1968, while Congress Hall was owned as part of a Cape May Bible Conference.*

With ghosts on the mind, my first thought after reading the passage dealt with the probabilities associated with a shipload of 425 passengers and treasure never seen again—or at least *mostly* never seen again. My thought: *Isn't Cape May the perfect place for these souls to reside and walk? They would certainly have enough accommodations.*

Looking more into the story, I found that there was much controversy around it. The *Juno* was hit by a terrible storm and began taking on water all those years ago. Luckily, there was a nearby American schooner, the *La Favorita*, who was able to take on seven of the survivors before the rest of the passengers, crew, and the ship were lost in the heavy fog. In horror, the sailors of the *La Favorita* were close enough to hear the ghastly cries for help as the boat disappeared beneath the water. It was estimated that at least 413 people died that night.

By dawn, all traces that the *Juno* and her passengers ever existed had been taken by the sea. And the silver? Twenty-three tons of it had sunk. (Crank up the camp fire—is this a story for the night, or what?) And worse still, years and years went by (until the 1990s) before the location of the ship was identified. *Shipwrecks in the Americas* by Robert Marx, published in 1983, states that the *Juno* sunk on October 29, 1802, near Cape May with 425 people and over 300,000 pesos in silver. Never to be found.

Another report says that a salvage company (Quicksilver) searched for ten years and maintained that some forty recovered items from the ship were found forty miles out to sea. Ben Benson of Sea Hunt Inc., however, reports that, in 1996, he pinpointed the skeleton of the wreck, partly buried in sand and mud about 1,500 feet from shore in twenty feet of water—near Assateague Island, Virginia.

Still another story tells of the *Juno* beginning to leak while near Bermuda (Bermuda Triangle fame) as it was heading north for repairs. Lost in the fog in the Bermuda Triangle...

Regardless of where the ship went down, its anchor has shown up on the lawn of Congress Hall and is now part of ghostly Cape May history. But what of the souls? Do they reside at the Hall as well; or are they strolling the Cape May streets wondering why no one came to meet them at the docks? Are the souls of the *Juno* frozen in time along with their treasures? No one knows...for sure.

### The Halls of Congress

The lovely and inspiring Congress Hall, built in 1816 as a wooden boarding house, is known as the nation's oldest seashore resort. But, like many of the hotels in Cape May, it suffered greatly when the ravages of fire struck in 1878. It was very fortunate that no lives were lost during this tragic property loss. Though it got its name from owner Thomas H. Hughes (in 1828) when he was elected to the U.S. Congress, the building's additional claim to fame is in its magnificent architecture—the hall being 200 feet long and 45 feet wide with 16-foot ceilings. (There are many places at the Congress for ghosts to roam.)

Certainly, the building itself was a vision, both outside and inside. It smacked of high class and wealthy customers—not in a bad way, but with a *stand-up-and-shout-I-belong-in-Cape-May-forever* kind of way. For, indeed, the trials that beset the seaside hotel over the years make its current stance a triumphant one.

Once we got beyond the 400 plus people that might be bound to the anchor outside, we took to roaming the building inside—incognito at first. We wanted to get a sense of the property's feel, its grasp on those that roamed the interior of it. One of the most striking nuances was the original black and white marble floor, but there were other architectural features that held the atmosphere securely in the past. The elevators (always a spooky place to be for me, as is fictionalized in my book, *Haunted Elevator*) were original, opening on both sides—with a habit of opening when no one was there to push the buttons. The hallways upstairs where the rooms were located were carpeted in a fashion where the wood could be seen on either side by the wall, and room doorways were slated doors (with a more secure interior door behind the slats). The room we visited brought to mind the word *beachy,* with walls painted in light blue and pastel trim throughout. Furniture was of apparent antique style, carpets were striped, and vanity tops were marble. The bathrooms were bright and airy with tiny black and white tiles for flooring.

This particular room overlooked the pool area (in old postcards, the pool was absent), and it appeared that the perfect party could be thrown right there on the Congress Hall lawn—or maybe a filming of a James Bond movie would be appropriate. Yes, it was quite elegant.

To be more realistic, I must say that this truly magnificent place was, in 1882, host to a young twenty-six year old John Phillip Sousa who was conducting for the Marine Merchant Band, there by special permission of the secretary of the Navy for a concert on the lawn. (A photograph hung prominently in the hallway announced that Sousa grew a beard to appear older as he performed for 3,000 people in attendance.) The point is that the number of folks in and out of this hotel over the years is staggering.

We quietly toured the building, slipping in and out of gift shops, and other public areas before we finally decided to talk with those working at the front desk. (You may be noting that I'm not mentioning any ghostly perceptions—my EMF meter was quiet and there were no interesting perceptions to feel for me.) At the front desk, two young ladies were quick to assure us that there were no ghosts that they'd come into contact with during their employment—nor had they ever heard of any.

But we knew better. Author Tina Skinner talked personally with Congress Hall's Executive Chef Jeffrey Klova, who had advised that people hear voices in the boiler room—with no one around. And there's a lock on the liquor cabinet downstairs where the wines and alcohol are kept—it swings for no reason. (He doesn't discount the air conditioner's vibration, but it has raised questions.)

Back to my visit, my husband and I made our way into a closed dining room, filled with tables for as long as the eye could see. The only light apparent was that from outside the tall windows, filtering in to touch a mass of white table cloths. The air felt heavy and a slight dizziness touched me—not intense like I felt at Elaine's, but there. I noted it, but continued to look around me.

In a smaller room that connected the hallway to the larger dining area stood a piece of furniture, a hutch of sorts, that displayed a mirror. We were standing still, talking about the air in the room when I noticed — from the corner of my eye — a quick movement. Then, it was gone. Had I not been looking for ghosts, I would've dismissed it as imagination. In fact, I still may be inclined to do so, for it was that sudden—there and gone. But whatever it was, it gave me a quick shiver and then the air in the room seemed to "lift", as if never heavy, but always light and fresh.

But I couldn't be sure. I'm leaving it at imagination for now.

Leaving that room, we went across the hallway to the bar and lounge. My EMF meter, within my wide-mouthed purse (so I could see it without anyone else seeing it), began flashing red in the bar area—and then stopped abruptly.

There were lots of customers enjoying the morning by lounging in the area, and we managed to stop one of the waiters for the ballroom as he came through waiting on clientele. I asked about ghosts. He immediately nodded. "Oh yes!" he said. It was common knowledge that one of the ladies sitting on the couch in the bar area could have sworn that someone touched her arm. He rushed away.

We walked to the couch; no response from the meter or our intuition. We walked about the grounds for awhile longer, but found no other strange phenomena or mysteries to unravel.

Other people have had or have known people who've experienced things at Congress Hall. Craig McManus tells of those who've encountered shadow figures, disembodied footsteps, and he's personally interacted with the spirit of a lady distraught by the fire in the gas lamps, as well as other residual encounters—lots of them. He's even gotten EVP readings that include strange noises and horses whining. Laurie Hull got the impression that it was haunted particularly by a child (Craig mentions this, as well).

Author Jennifer Brownstone Kopp and friend Leigh Ann Austin were having lunch at Congress Hall one afternoon with a psychic friend, Gail (last name unknown), who saw spirits in full garb; Gail especially saw women in the Hall wearing the long dresses of the eighteenth century, complete with parasol. On this one occasion, such a woman beaconed Gail to follow her. It was apparent that the spirit wanted to tell her something. Stopping near the lobby, the spirit pointed, but there was nothing there. Gail was frustrated more when the spirit vanished.

The next day, though, things became clearer. A fire broke out in the very place that the spirit had been pointing to. The spirit had been trying to warn Gail. When asked by her friends whether this kind of warning was a typical thing, she replied with an answer that I've heard throughout ghost hunting and while interpreting the tarot. "Yes, it is common. I try awful hard to understand, but I can't always." It comes down to interpretation; one person's view of a message may be entirely different than another's. She felt that if she had understood the message, she could have warned the owners of Congress Hall—but it was fortunate that little damage was done.

When it comes down to it, though, I don't think it matters whether or not ghosts currently reside at Congress Hall. The elegance of the Hall and its interesting and tragic historical background provides enough mystery for ghostly thoughts and fun times.

# Chapter Seven
# Hotel Macomber

727 Beach Avenue
Cape May, NJ 08204
609-884-3020
http://www.hotelmacomber.com/

---

Directions: Go South on the New Jersey Garden State Parkway to Exit 0. Continue straight onto Route 109 and over the large bridge. Continue over the small flat bridge and bear left to the beaches. At the stop sign turn left and bear right onto Pittsburgh Avenue. Continue on Pittsburgh to the beach. Turn Right onto Beach Avenue.

---

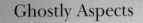

## Ghostly Aspects

- *Sounds of moving items*
- *Drawers opening and shutting by themselves*
- *Beds messed up*
- *Lights on and off*
- *Clocks stopping and starting*
  *(or running fast or slow)*
- *Feeling of a presence*
- *Woman in Victorian garb*

### Transforming Ghosts

The Hotel Macomber, a family-run shingle-style hotel, has a beautiful presence that time cannot extinguish. The last building in Cape May to become a historic landmark, it is the largest frame structure east of the Mississippi River, per their website. The Union Park Restaurant, as well as gift shops, can also be taken advantage of while visiting this grand hotel.

Laurie Hull's visit to the Hotel Macomber turned up some interesting specters—and theories about the ghosts of this lovely building. She immediately pointed my attention to the second floor window (which can be seen on the photo shown on her ghostly website: http://www.delcoghosts.com/). This, she's heard from those at the hotel, is where people feel the presence of ethereal activity. It was there that people would find drawers were opening and closing on their own volition in the middle of the night, beds were being disarranged after being nicely made, and lights would go on and off without human hands to flip the switches. There's also been a woman in Victorian-like clothing seen as well.

The interesting thing about this second floor room is that there is a very large power transformer right outside the window. One theory is that electromagnetic energy assists ghosts in their manifestation—or ghostly behavior. "With all this electricity right there next to that room, it cannot be a coincidence that it is *THE* most haunted room in the hotel. It has to have something to do with it. They can draw right from this electricity—its right there," Laurie said.

We talked at length about electromagnetic energy, since this affects spirit phenomena greatly—the same things were of interest in the bar area at Elaine's. She advised that the effects that EMF energy has on some people can be compared to people who are sensitive to changes in the weather or the barometric pressure; some are aware of it, some are not. (This put it in perfect perspective for me because I'm one of the people affected by weather changes—my sinuses act up furiously when rain is on its way in. This also explained to me the light-headedness and dizziness I felt at Elaine's. I was responding to the electromagnetic energy in the area—the same energy that the ghosts were drawing to manifest their activity.) Laurie mentioned again that, if someone is sensitive to it, it may feel like a cold breeze going by if it's at a high enough level. Additionally, if high enough, a person can feel disoriented (I'd seen this happen to a member in my own ghost group during an investigation at the Eastern State Penitentiary in Philadelphia), dizzy, anxious, panicky—several varied reactions that can affect people's perceptions. In Laurie's group, Delaware County Paranormal Research, a construction expert is on the team. His job: identifying specific sources of electromagnetic currents prior to an investigation.

At any rate, Laurie found it interesting that the ghostly activity was so intent in this one area and that nearby, a power transformer was there to possibly aid in its manifestation. "If you are a person who is sensitive to that, you could be seeing things that aren't there just because of the electromagnetic energy ...So why in this room? You know that if people stayed in this room or worked in this room or are affected by it [electromagnetic energy], they probably would experience things."

It sounded to me like Laurie was saying that the electromagnetic energy was making people see things that were not there. "Well," I said, "electromagnetic energy is not going to open drawers and such..."

"No, it's not; but if there *is* a ghost in there, it would be very strong because of the electromagnetic energy available. If you're buying the theory that ghosts take magnetic energy from batteries, and people, and the earth, it's going to have a huge source right there to do whatever it wants to do—which could open drawers. That's why the ghost is probably so active. Most people think that it's connected. I've always wondered what would happen if they moved the transformer box—what would happen? If it was my hotel, that's what I would do—just to see! ...if they moved it to another area, would that area become haunted?"

As ghost hunters will do, Laurie (along with her Mom) went on the area ghost tour to see what they had to say about the Macomber. The evening was dark and they were standing out in front of the hotel listening to the tour guide talk about the paranormal experiences that had been reported there over the years. It was then that Laurie noticed the transformer and noted its close proximity to the haunted room in question — and just as she noticed it, the transformer went *POP*, causing sparks to fly out ... this was at the exact moment that the guide was talking about the premise that electromagnetic energy had a connection to the activity in the room.

Laurie's mother said, "Did you see that?!"

Laurie was nonplussed. "I know that it's coincidental, but I've also noticed that in my experience of investigating the paranormal, the experience of coincidence increases exponentially when you go into a haunted place. And *that* can't be a coincidence... Everything is connected. Everything *knows* what everything else is doing on some level in the universe."

I certainly agree with this thinking from my own experiences with the paranormal.

### Happily Visiting Room 10

But to move on to the hauntings, much activity has been reported to happen in Room 10 at the Macomber. There are guests who have reported the feeling of a ghostly presence in that room is so strong that it is uncomfortable for them. I'm thinking that it doesn't help to have drawers opening and closing without human help during the night, or to have the lights go off and on without real hands to flip the switch. Clocks, too, have been noted to either start or stop running—or run fast or slow—in this room.

Laurie said that the activity in the room has been linked to a widow who visited the hotel a few times a year after her husband died. "Apparently, she was so happy there, she continued to visit even after she died."

Haunted New Jersey is another premier ghost group with a tour that has for many years serviced Cape May and won such awards as "Best Tour in Cape May" by readers of www.capemay.com's Internet magazine. They not only tell the stories, but educate visitors about hauntings and ghost hunting techniques—they are true researchers. This group takes pride in the fact that they don't look at isolated incidents as they research, but rather the building blocks of a haunting. From the group's promotional materials regarding the Macomber:

> *The Hotel comes complete with its share of ghostly visitors including an object throwing poltergeist, a man who makes animal sounds, a waitress who choked on a chicken bone, and a woman who still vacations there some fifty years after her death!*

I'd say that these ghostly visitors may be worth visiting! (Find out more about New Jersey's haunts and this professional group at www.hauntednewjersey.com.)

# Chapter Eight
# Cabanna's Beach Bar and Grill

429 Beach Avenue
Cape May, NJ 08204
(609) 884-4800
http://www.cabanasonthebeach.com

---

Directions: Take the Garden State Parkway south
and follow it to Exit 0, where it intersects with Route
109. Go straight and follow it over the big bridge at
the Cape May Harbor. When you enter town you will
be on Lafayette Street. Turn left onto Decatur Street,
then right onto Beach Avenue.

---

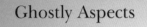

## Ghostly Aspects

- *A woman waiting…*
- *Lights off and on*
- *Locks unlocking*
- *Bulbs popping*
- *EMF activity*
- *Temperature variations*
- *Feelings*

### Spirits for the Spirits!

Though it may sound as though the only haunts in Cape May are found in the hotel industry, this is not true. A ghost, just like the rest of us, can have its head turned by a fun-filled lively atmosphere, good food, and maybe even some spirits (of the drinking kind). And where could such a spirit find such an atmosphere to reside?

Cabanna's.

On my fact-finding visit to Cape May, accompanied by my photographer husband, we stopped into Cabanna's not to ghost hunt, but to have some lunch. But in the ghost hunting world, things never seem to go as planned. The EMF meter I had in my purse started pulsing red the moment I walked into the bar—and didn't stop the whole time we were there. I was self-conscious at first. Would the other customers notice my purse flashing? Yes, I could've turned the thing off, but I was entranced by the incredible spikes of activity.

We started immediately to look at power sources and locations as though we were graphing a ghost investigation. Finally, still hungry, we sat at the bar to order food. (Special note: If you're a ghost hunter, always sit at the bar. No one you meet will have as much information or provide as many leads as your bartender. The bartenders of the world have their fingers on the pulse of the world.) George Kelly, moonlighting from his job as a high/middle school English teacher, was no exception. Friendly and down-to-earth, he was kind enough to illuminate the ghostly stories that enriched Cabanna's.

The first things that he talked about were how people tended to hear, see, and feel things while they were working at the restaurant/lounge; and that there were a lot of changes in temperature inside the establishment—sometimes the air being more cold on the inside than the outside even if the heat was on. "I've felt a sudden chill. And I'm not all that sensitive to this kind of thing—I'm kind of a skeptic," said George. "I've never *seen* a ghost, so I try to balance it. But there are just things that happen here … things that can't be explained."

He added that there was little activity on the first floor. (My husband and I just glanced at each other with raised eyebrows and then down to my flashing purse sitting open on the floor at our feet.) He also said that there were so many people in and out that, when strange things occurred, they were often dismissed. He personally knew of weird noises, locks that are locked one moment and unlocked the next, lights that went on and off, a working light switch suddenly not working…

There are four floors (a restaurant on the second floor—Martini Beach) with the majority of activity taking place on the third, which is used for storage. "Bizarre things happen from time to time," said George. "The locks here are good … they [the ghosts] just like to lock and unlock them. The lights have to be checked out all the time, too. Especially the fluorescent ones. For some reason the florescent lights dim and we've had bulbs explode. That's always happening. Nobody's actually been around; you hear it, then go to check, and then just see what happens."

I asked if these things happened when other people were there as opposed to just when employees were closing up. "Oh yeah, absolutely," he said. "It's just a question of whether you are conscious of it and able to attend to it, or if you are just preoccupied and need to go about your business. When you are working, you really don't pay any attention to it. It just doesn't dawn on you."

"We hear stories even here at Cabanna's about people being lost at sea and then returning to haunt our location," George added. "But those stories seem to be told at every place in Cape May. It's an old waling town, a fishing village. Then along comes a story of a widow who has lost her husband at sea—a tortured soul. Could it happen? Absolutely. There are definitely men who were lost at sea back in the 1800s and 1900s. As far as actually who it *is* doing the haunting is very blurry. I would think it's just one particular ghost that's more attached to the actual building and the house than anything else."

George Kelly was not the only person who has had experiences with ghostly phenomena at Cabanna's. I spoke with the wife of Anthony Barra, a former employee of the restaurant, Martini Beach, located on the second floor. Mrs. Barra said that Anthony is quite the skeptic when it comes to the paranormal, but I think that even he has had to rethink his beliefs after hearing the story she had to tell me! His tale relates to a particular woman who is fairly well-known (i.e., *seen*!), waiting for her son. It seems that her son died, killed by the train that used to come through that very location. So she is now there, at Cabanna's, waiting for her son who never came back.

One night, while Anthony was working, this ghostly woman came to visit. He was sitting at the bar, counting the money for the evening and no one was around. Suddenly, he saw a woman in her thirties go into the bathroom. This was not an unusual event, obviously, but he knew that he'd have to wait for her to come out before he could close for the night. He waited and waited for her. Thinking this was a customer who might have been sick or drunk, he waited for her for quite some time. But she didn't come out.

Finally, when he tired of waiting to close the establishment, he investigated the bathroom to see if she was all right. No one was there. This was a distressing thing because he knew there was a person there. He'd seen her!

Laurie Hull and I visited Cabanna's (also for a bite to eat) after spending the day with the ghosts at Elaine's. We were hoping to have an encounter or two while there. This afternoon the restaurant and lounge on the first floor was filled with people. Even George was too busy to talk about any interesting recent encounters.

The noise level was quite high, as well. Laurie, being clairaudient, hears things as though coming from a static-like radio transmission. This was not a good atmosphere to pick up that kind of activity. She received no impressions during our lunch—and, oddly enough, my EMF meter did not register at all during our visit. Cabanna's was definitely ghost-free on this fine afternoon.

But we all know, ghosts come and ghosts go! (You don't think the woman's son finally showed, do you?)

## Chapter Nine
# Quickie Cape May Haunts

The following haunts were the results of quick visits or interactions involving haunted locations in Cape May. Most of the stories below are much more elaborate in reality, but hopefully, these snippets will encourage you to find out more about these wonderful places!

## The Atlantic Book Store

500 Washington Street Mall
Cape May, NJ 08204
(609) 898-9694
http://www.atlanticbooks.us/

---

Directions: Take the Garden State Parkway south and follow it to Exit 0, where it intersects with Route 109. Go straight and follow it over the big bridge at the Cape May Harbor. When you enter town you will be on Lafayette Street. Turn left onto Ocean Street and then right onto Washington Street to the mall.

---

*Ghostly Aspects: Activity in basement and children's area; EMF readings*

### Never Judge a Book by it's...Ghost

Being both a representative of my publisher and an author of creepy books of all kinds, whenever I visit a shopping area, I visit the bookshop to say *hello*. Atlantic Books was on my list of stops this day—not for ghostly research, but to introduce myself and to see if there was anything they needed or wanted to talk about in the book world. Always in "ghost mode," however, I made my project part of my introduction and, to my surprise, I found that Atlantic Books was haunted.

Store employee Rochelle Eldredge said that the ghostly folks in question were named Kennedy and they inhabited the basement and the children's room area. She advised that this particular location used to be a pharmacy and that (Craig McMannus, psychic medium) had visited, telling them that he'd had a vision of the pouring of pharmaceuticals. We did step back to the children's area, where I found the EMF readings were just under 3—a good sign—all the way up to spikes of 6. Of course, there were many electrical items that might be affecting such a reading—I just wasn't sure. The interesting part was that the energy seemed to move. In one place I would get a positive reading, but seconds later, all would be quiet in the same location. Best left to another day!

(Craig has many interactive tales to tell about this trendy little book shop in *Book 2* of *The Ghosts of Cape May.*)

◇◇◇◇◇◇◇◇◇◇◇◇◇◇◇◇◇

# The Peter Shields Inn

1301 Beach Drive
Cape May, NJ  08204
(609) 884-9090 or 800-355-6565
http://www.petershieldsinn.com/

---

Directions: Follow the Garden State Parkway into Cape May and turn left at Sidney Street, left again at Washington Street, and right at the traffic island. Follow Pittsburgh Avenue to Beach Drive and turn right. The Peter Shields is located at the corner of Beach and Trenton avenues.

---

*Ghostly Aspects: Lights on and off mysteriously; Man in the bathroom; Feelings of a presence*

### A Lady's Man at the Inn

Peter Shields, according to Jack Wright, author of *Tommy's Folly* (a book that tells the story of Congress Hall), was a real estate developer and president of the Cape May Real Estate Company. Quite charming, this businessman, hailing from Pittsburgh, was the star of Cape May. During Shields' involvement with the Congress Hall project, his fifteen-year-old son shot himself in a hunting accident—a terrible blow. Though he'd planned on turning the beach community into the new Newport, things were just not developing as he'd planned. Finally, in 1912, Shields and his family packed their things and left their beautiful homestead on Beach Drive.

According to the Delaware County Paranormal Research group, this stately home went through several transitions before becoming the acclaimed Peter Shields Inn in 1989. At one time, it was known as the Cape May Tuna Club; at other points, it was a transcendental mediation center, a gambling club, and a brothel.

Of course, with all the turmoil, it's no surprise that some believe that Peter Shields never left his Cape May home. It has been reported that the lights go off mysteriously for no reason and that a young man (some say Shields) can be seen roaming along the halls or on the stairs. This phantom has been seen often in the hall by the ladies room, but most guests have reported feeling a presence that might be of a paranormal nature happening as soon as they've entered the inn. It's been said, too, that this young male ghost has an eye for the women and that it is more likely to appear to them than the visiting men.

When she talked with the owner, Laurie Hull was told that, for some reason, this male ghost is seen always in the ladies room. Laurie said that this was probably because the ladies room was a room that he used to store things in—and *not* a bathroom. The owner advised that because the inn had gone through so many incarnations, he wasn't sure how the room was originally used. Laurie had a feeling that the space was a bigger area and was possibly some kind of room like a study or office—some place the ghost may have spent time when he was living. "He just isn't seeing it as a ladies room!" she said.

*Laurie added that bathrooms often tend to be haunted. "It's said that water is also connected somehow to spirit activity. Places where there is a lot of water running through—underground streams, etc.—seem to see increases in the levels of paranormal activity. I'm not sure what the connection is, but islands are always haunted; and the more inland you get, it seems the less activity is noted—unless there are a lot of rivers or underground streams in the area. Water is a great conductor of energy. It's another theory—it's not been proven, though."*

◇◇◇◇◇◇◇◇◇◇◇◇◇◇◇◇

# John F. Craig House

609 Columbia Avenue
Cape May, NJ 08204
(609) 884-0100 or (877) 544-0314
http://www.johnfcraig.com

---

Directions: Take the Garden State Parkway south and follow it to Exit 0, where it intersects with Route 109. Go straight and follow it over the big bridge at the Cape May Harbor. When you enter town you will be on Lafayette Street. Follow it to the First Traffic Light at Madison Avenue. Turn left on Madison and go to the blue Water Tower at the intersection of Columbia and Madison. Turn right on Columbia and follow it about six blocks and just beyond the war memorial is the Craig House on your right. (One building from the corner of Columbia Avenue and Ocean Street.)

---

*Ghostly Aspects: A seamstress ghost; Presence in Room 2; Red-headed Girl; Footsteps; Moving things; Doors opening*

### It "Seams" to Me, There's a Ghost!

The Craig House Bed and Breakfast was built in 1866, and was initially two houses combined to make one. There was a pre-1850s house moved and attached at the current location to the new Victorian house being built. Some of the construction is early Cape May in style with lower ceilings, while others reflect the years that the Craig family used the property as a summer cottage. It was an apartment house until the 1980s when it became an inn. Almost right away the innkeepers received reports of ghostly activity!

When Laurie Hull visited the hotel, she immediately felt the presence of a woman and she was fairly certain that a man was reported there, as well—though she didn't feel his presence on this visit. The lady ghost was seemingly taking care of everything there (the house), keeping things in order. The owners told her that though they'd not *seen* anything, they *felt* things. And little things would happen, like doors being open when they thought they'd been closed, footsteps, things being moved around after they'd been cleaned up, and things put down one place and being found in another shortly after.

"The spirit here wants to stay," says Laurie. "It's her house. Let her stay. She's attached to it." This psychic feels very strongly about doing what's right for the spirit involved.

Another story told to Laurie involved a female guest who reported that after spending the night in Room 2 (the Lucy Johnson Room on the second floor in the 1850s section), she came down to thank the owner for sewing a button onto her trousers. But, of course, the owner had done no such service for the guest. The story went that the guest had actually left a needle and thread out to sew the button herself but had not had the opportunity—nor had anyone else. Yet, the deed was done...

◇◇◇◇◇◇◇◇◇◇◇◇◇◇◇◇◇◇

# The Thorn and the Rose

822 Stockton Avenue
Cape May, NJ  08204
(609) 884-8142
http://www.thornandtherose.com/index.html

Directions: Take the Garden State Parkway (Route 109) and continue south as it turns into Lafayette Street. Take a left onto Madison and a right onto Stockton Avenue to the Thorn and the Rose on the left side of the street.

*Ghostly Aspects: French-speaking ghost; French-speaking mortals; cold spots; Feelings of Fire; Sounds of Jacks and balls bouncing*

### A Hot Time in the Old Town Tonight!

The Thorn and the Rose is noted for being the first seashore resort in America, beginning their lovely Victorian service in 1761 (though it was extensively renovated in the 1990s). "This place is really cool," said Laurie Hull. (Though it's true that the inn is very beautiful, I think she might be referring to its ghosts!)

A specific interesting (and contemporary) haunting was related to me and apparently happened when the establishment first opened for business. The owners were said to have been pulled from their sleep one night by a female guest banging on their door, complaining that there was a ghost in her room! The owners, of course, went with the woman to check out the situation, but other than the cold chill of the room, they saw nothing unusual. The woman insisted that not only was the ghost there, but that it was speaking French—and that *she* was speaking French too! And, she didn't speak French.

Then, the owner's young son stepped into the room to see what all the commotion was—and *he* began speaking French! (Needless to say, the child did not speak French.) They removed him from the room, putting him back to bed. In the morning, he had no recollection of the event.

The woman seeing the phenomena advised that there were three spirits in the room; she held an impromptu séance to find out what was happening and identified a small child and two sisters there at the Thorn and the Rose. She also mentioned that one of the ghosts had been killed on the other side of the home by someone close.

Laurie didn't feel the three spirits when she visited. Rather, she felt as though there was a spirit of a woman there. She didn't feel the small child or the two sisters. Her feelings manifested as someone being abandoned or left—and that she was still waiting for someone to come back.

An anonymous woman talked about staying at the Thorn and the Rose in 2002. She and her husband heard the sounds of jacks and bouncing balls all night, but what really unnerved them was when her husband began to speak fluent French. Additionally, they could see lights on all over the third floor when they knew that the inn was empty except for them that night. She added that when the owner took them on a tour of the main house, "I felt like my body was on fire and I almost fainted."

Still nothing threatening has ever occurred in this lovely bed and breakfast. But maybe, if you want to learn a new language…or play some jacks…

◇◇◇◇◇◇◇◇◇◇◇◇◇◇◇◇

# The Washington Inn

801 Washington Street
Cape May, NJ 08204
(609) 884-5697
http://www.washingtoninn.com

---

Directions: Take the Garden State Parkway South, one mile past city limit sign, turn left on to Jefferson Street. The Washington Inn is on the corner of Washington and Jefferson Streets.

---

*Ghostly Aspects: Staircase activity; Name calling*

### I Know You Are, But What Am I?

Originally a private residence, this lovely inn was built in 1840 as a Plantation home. It's been through many changes and renovations to enhance its charm. In 1940, it opened as an inn (run by Martha Hand and her daughter). Currently, the inn is run by the Craig family.

The last time Laurie Hull was there for a visit was during one of these renovation periods. She found that most of the ghostly activity was taking place right at the entrance. It seems that there used to be a stairway there, but it was taken out for the purpose of turning the building from a home to a hotel. In fact, the inside was completely redone to make it the charismatic inn it is today.

But ever since the stairs came out, something else seems to have come in! And it all happens at the entryway where the stairs *used* to be. Somebody didn't want the stairs moved. One of the reports of paranormal interest is that people say they can hear their own names being called in that area. Laurie felt that this was a woman, and whoever she was, she does not understand where her stairs have gone. Speculating that this may have been the woman's house, and these were the stairs she used all the time, she may be wondering why they are no longer available for use.

Laurie kindly advised the owners that it might be a good idea for them to actually tell their ghost that the building is a hotel now and that they are just trying to take care of it. "Tell the ghost that a lot of people are going to come to see the house and that they are going to think that it's beautiful. She doesn't need to worry about the stairs—there are other stairs to use now." Kinda ghostly psychology, the way I see it.

◇◇◇◇◇◇◇◇◇◇◇◇◇◇◇◇

# The Columns by the Sea

1513 Beach Avenue
Cape May, NJ 08204
(609) 884-2228
http://www.colvmnscapemay.com/about.html

---

Directions: Take the Garden State Parkway into Cape May. The Parkway turns into Lafayette Street. Follow Lafayette and turn left onto Sidney Avenue. Turn left onto Washington Street, right onto Texas Avenue and stay straight to go onto Pittsburgh Avenue. Turn left onto Beach Avenue to Columns by the Sea.

---

*Ghostly Aspects: Footsteps overhead; Figure on a bed; Impressions on a bed; Strange Mirror and wet walls; Doors opening and closing; Moving baby carriage*

## Here's Lookin' at You, Kid...

The lovely Renaissance Revival architectural wonder of Columns by the Sea is known as the first home to be built on the eastern end of the beachfront in

Cape May, taking two years to construct. Dr. Charles Davis and wife Emily built it as a summer retreat home for them and their nine children; there are twenty-three rooms for ghosts to roam in this bed and breakfast styled after the grand palazzos of the Italian Riviera. It was sold in the 1940s, becoming an apartment house; and then in the early 1980s, this home became the well-known bed and breakfast, having grand success ever since.

When Laurie Hull first went to visit this unique and luxurious place, she was told that, at times, people heard footsteps overhead when no one was there. But that's not why she was there. She'd heard through the ghostly grapevine that the Columns by the Sea had a very mysterious mirror.

Located in the main parlor, water supposedly appeared not only on the mirror face, but on the walls near this antique treasure. On the day she visited, not much was said to her in the way of hauntings. And there was no indication of water on or around the mirror. But Laurie did get a weird feeling around the mirror.

"It was like...something else was there, something you couldn't see." She described the feeling as being inside a library and knowing that you are not alone there, yet no one is within your sight. You have the feeling that someone is behind you or around the isle. You know if you just walk around that isle, you'll see them. "There's a presence of another person there—nothing evil or anything like that. But definitely, something attached to that mirror. I've spent a lot of time looking in them, and they do capture images to some degree."

Too, people have talked about doors opening on their own, and even an antique wicker baby carriage that has been known to move by itself.

All in all, a luxurious place to hunt a haunt!

◇◇◇◇◇◇◇◇◇◇◇◇◇◇◇◇◇

# The Victorian Lace Inn

901 Stockton Avenue
Cape May, NJ 08204
(609) 884-1772
http://www.victorianlaceinn.com

Directions: Take the Garden State Parkway into Cape May. The Parkway turns into Lafayette Street. Follow Lafayette Street to Madison Street. Make a left on Madison. Make a right on Stockton Avenue.

*Ghostly Aspects: Footsteps; Furniture movement; Items disappear, then reappear*

### Now Ya See it, Now Ya Don't!

Cindy Starr-Whitman, investigator for the Chester County Paranormal Research Society, and her husband, Frank, remember a lovely trip to Cape May and the beautiful Victorian Lace Inn. They stayed in a two-bedroom suite on the third floor in this unique bed and breakfast with a chimney staircase and custom stained glass windows (designed by the innkeeper!). Carol was thrilled that they could see the ocean from their bedroom, and surprised that they heard ghostly footsteps and heard things moving around when no one was there! She also mentioned that when things are cleaned up or put away, suddenly, they appear again!

# Chapter Ten
# Other Creepy Places!

The places listed in this chapter have either been reported as haunted, rumored as haunted, or are just generally creepy. A more detailed investigation is forthcoming in future haunted book editions—but for now, you just might like to do some ghost hunting of your own!

## The Cape May Puffin

32 Jackson Street
Cape May, NJ 08204
(609) 884-2664
http://www.capemaypuffin.com/rose.html

Ghostly Aspects: Spirits in the building, EMF readings, EVPs, orb photography
Visit www.southjerseyghostresearch.org for details

◇◇◇◇◇◇◇◇◇◇◇◇◇◇◇◇◇

# The Angel of the Sea

5 Trenton Avenue
Cape May, NJ 08204
(609) 884-3369
http://www.angelofthesea.com/

Ghostly Aspects: Vibrating beds, swaying furniture, lights and televisions turning off and on, strange photographs

◇◇◇◇◇◇◇◇◇◇◇◇◇◇◇◇

# Poverty Beach

It's located at the Extreme East end of the beaches at Cape May, at the end of Beach Drive.

Ghostly Aspects: evil water spirit—man in a black cloak, black beard and horrible black eyes seen floating in the air

◇◇◇◇◇◇◇◇◇◇◇◇◇◇◇◇

# The Brass Bed Inn

719 Columbia Avenue
Cape May, New Jersey 08204
(609) 884-2302
http://www.capemayviews.com/Hotels/TheBrass-
BedInn/The-Brass-Bed-Inn.htm

Ghostly Aspects: Ghostly Confederate Civil War
Soldier standing by the bed

### The Witches League of Cape May

This is a secret-ish organization, so initial contacts
need to be made through their website at: http://cov-
enantofrhiannon.faithweb.com/capemay.htm.

Ghostly Aspect: No real ghosts, but interesting…

# Chapter Eleven
# On the Beaches of Cape May

## Higbee Beach

http://www.capemaybeaches.com/cmb_higbee-beach.php

---

Directions: Travel to the end of New England Road, on the Delaware Bay. Make a left from Bayshore Road and follow to the end. The beach is about four miles from the city of Cape May and about three miles from the Hawk Watch platform at Cape May Point.

---

Ghostly Aspects:

- *Man and dog on beach*
- *Pirates*
- *Disappearing walker*
- *Master and slave*

### Ahoy, Mates (Said the Parrot—I Mean Warbler)

Higbee Beach is a "Wildlife Management Area" for the New Jersey Department of Environmental Protection, Division of Fish, Game, and Wildlife and probably the perfect place in all of North America to see fall migrating warblers (for those not in the know, warblers are birds). The beach is a stopover for migrating hawks, songbirds, and wintering birds.

But perhaps they should add ghosts to their protective measures. With a diversity of habitats and the close proximity to the peninsula, not only is it great for birding, but for ghosting as well.

It's not the main beach in Cape May—you actually have to make an effort to go there, but perfect for watching birds and considering ghosts. Laurie Hull said that once there, there is a specified path that must be navigated rather than someone having the full run of the grass or other marked areas. Laurie visited there prior to going on one of the local ghost tours where she gleaned more information that placed questions in her mind.

You see, this was the very first area in Cape May that she'd been to—and she's been all over this quaint little town—where she actually felt there were pirates.

*"It was weird. All your life you're hearing of pirates up and down the East Coast. But this is the first place I've been in New Jersey where I feel like there actually were pirates—here, on this beach. I can see it in my mind. There*

*were pirates here. The ghost tour said no pirates, but I know they were all up and down this beach...pirates. I've heard that there were pirates in Wildwood, Martha's Hook, in Newport Rhode Island; I've never felt there were pirates here until I was on Higbee Beach...Even though I can't find proof saying they were on this particular beach...But it was right in my mind that there were pirates here.*

*When you go in a certain place, you get an idea. Sometimes its just an idea that's in your head, but you know its from the place—it's not from you. It's so hard to describe how this happens. When I went onto that beach, it just popped into my head that there were pirates there. It was a thought that came to my head...I could see them coming up on the beach, in a small boat, and they were looking around... I could just feel that they were pirates. It was so clear in my mind what was going on...I don't know if it was real—it could've been my imagination—but I've never felt that anywhere. I know that they were there. I also know that they weren't supposed to be there. And of all the places in New Jersey, this is the only place I've felt it. I think that not a lot of people go to this area, so maybe it's residual and it just hasn't been walked over by a hundred other energies that may have covered it up."*

She did confirm, however, that the popular *ghosts* of Higbee Beach are not pirates. Rather, the beach is supposed to be haunted by a man and his dog; though she didn't see either when she was there. Another version of the haunting identifies Mr. Higbee (thus Higbee Beach) as the ghost, and still another, a slave of Mr. Higbee who keeps a vigil at the grave of his master. Laurie added that she gets a very eerie feeling here, especially in the autumn.

Corinna (last name not used), a friend and work associate of Laurie's, said that when she was walking on the beach, she saw someone walking toward her, but her attention was on the water. When she pulled her attention back to the approaching person, there was no one there. Laurie reminded me that since you are not allowed to walk on the grass, there is no way that a person could be out of sight in that short moment. Corinna did not see a dog, however—only what she thought to be a man.

(It might be a good idea, too, to follow the advice of the posted signs and stay away from 9 p.m. till 5 a.m. …)

◇◇◇◇◇◇◇◇◇◇◇◇◇◇◇◇◇◇◇

# The Cape May Lighthouse

*http://www.state.nj.us/dep/parksandforests/parks/capemay.html*

---

Directions: The lighthouse is in the Cape May Point State Park, located off the southern end of the Garden State Parkway. Cross over Cape May Bridge onto Lafayette Street. At the intersection, bear right onto County Route 606 (Sunset Boulevard), then left onto Lighthouse Avenue. From Route 9, take County Route 626, Seashore Road and cross the bridge. For information on tours and hours of operation call: The Mid Atlantic Center for the Arts at (609) 884-5404.

Ghostly Aspects:

• *Spirits of former keepers and their families*

### Not Foggy Today...

I couldn't bring myself to climb the 217 steps from the ground to the top of this beautiful lighthouse. Just couldn't do it. Yes, it's entirely possible that I was thinking that the feat was a daunting one, or it could've been that nagging remembrance of the movie, *The Fog* (the old one, of course, where one of the final scenes takes place at the top of just such a lighthouse—at night, in the fog, with ghosts). Whatever the reason, my husband and I decided to read the brochure and talk to Rich, the very likeable attendant.

Rich was straight to the point. "I don't know about the kind of spirit you're talking about," he said when asked about ghostly activity, "but there is a certain kind of spirit to the place. It has its own atmosphere and ambiance."

I wondered about that feeling. "It's the character, the beauty, and the fact that it's here. People like the building, they like the reason for it, the way it looks. There's something fascinating about the light at night. It's sort of like something that lives. That's what I feel about it."

And he was right. Even in the bright of day, there was a life to this charismatic 157-foot-high lighthouse. But whatever ghosts inhabited this historic monument, seemed to be quiet this day, and I felt no intrusion of ghostly phenomena—my EMF meter remained still and my feelings normal. The brochure, however, speaks to ghosts of several former keepers and their families encountered by psychic medium Craig Mc-Mannus—so don't write off this ghostly beacon!

◇◇◇◇◇◇◇◇◇◇◇◇◇◇◇◇◇◇◇

# The Cape May Point Bunker

Directions: The bunker is adjacent to the lighthouse located in the Cape May Point State Park, located off the southern end of the Garden State Parkway. Cross over Cape May Bridge onto Lafayette Street. At the intersection, bear right onto County Route 606 (Sunset Boulevard), then left onto Lighthouse Avenue. From Route 9, take County Route 626, Seashore Road and cross the bridge.

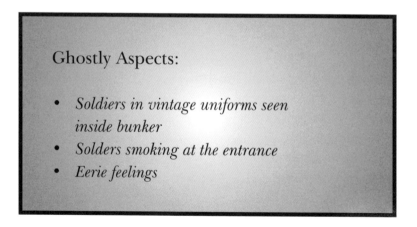

Ghostly Aspects:

- *Soldiers in vintage uniforms seen inside bunker*
- *Solders smoking at the entrance*
- *Eerie feelings*

## A Sandy Grave

Not far from the Cape May Lighthouse—just across the parking lot and down onto the beach—sits the Cape May

Point Bunker, a menacing structure that sits in the middle of the sand like a huge derelict monolith. It was built by the U.S. Army Corps of Engineers when World War II first broke out and was initially hidden by sand, necessary for such spying requirements. This monstrous beast would have been the last line of offense if the war would have taken a turn for the worse. Luckily, this was not the case.

Still, there are those who have said that the war is not over for the ghostly figures who have been seen moving around inside this structure. People talk about men in uniforms of old peering out from abandoned gun ports and of soldiers standing at the entrances smoking their cigarettes.

A sunny afternoon, we saw no such soldiers, yet there was an eerieness we felt the closer we came to the bunker. There was nothing there…but there was *something* there…a shiver reached me like that of creeping flesh—starting slowly and then turning aggressive at shoulder level. Yes, this was a creepy place.

A good place to visit, but I wouldn't want to smoke there.

◇◇◇◇◇◇◇◇◇◇◇◇◇◇◇◇◇

# Any Place on the Beaches of Cape May

> Ghostly Aspects:
>
> • *Disappearing Woman Ghost*

## The Poor Shimmering Woman

Of course, there's the story you hear everywhere you go when in a beach town. I heard it several times, with little variation beyond the beach the story belonged to. It goes like this: A young man and woman were sitting on the beach watching the ocean—off season (or in season, or no season). They see a figure emerge from the water. It's a woman dressed in Victorian dress—shimmering and iridescent. She stops. She turns to look at them and stares. Then turns to look back to look at the water and then slowly fades.

True? Possibly, happening some place on a Cape May beach but moved and changed over the years of telling—now a story for any beach. Urban legend? Very possible, too, with some basis in truth and years of exaggeration or fantasy. Still, if you happen to see such a woman on the Cape May beaches, know that there are those who will say that you won't be the first…

# Chapter Twelve
# Thoughts of Psychic Laurie Hull

Throughout my research and time spent with Laurie, we often spoke of things paranormally related that did not relate exactly to the ghost stories told here, but still gave some insight into this controversial subject and how it applied to any location visited. For example, I wanted to know why she felt that some of the ghosts we'd encountered bothered to hang around Cape May (or any other location for that matter).

*"Well, some of them can't accept that they are dead and others may be very attached to material things and can't let go. Some stay around because they have something they've wanted to do and it didn't get done before their deaths. There's a million reasons—as many reasons as people have to do anything. Some spirits stay because they want to get back at somebody. Some stay because they are afraid of seeing someone on the other side. Some are afraid of going to hell on the other side."*

I found myself cringing at some of the reasons she was relating, as I was thinking of other investigations I'd been on personally—especially the Eastern State Penitentiary in Philadelphia—where the spirits managed to give much of their remorse or violent feelings to the investigators at hand. Reasons to stay behind are varied, yes, but possibly something that needs to be considered prior to visiting a particular location.

Laurie continued: "You just have to talk to them. I say *talk*, but it's more in your mind—it goes back and forth. And I've gotten in the habit of saying everything out loud because [as investigators] we want to get everything on tape. But since they [those people physically at the location] can't hear the ghost, I have to say what the ghosts say as well as what I say."

I'd had much experience now with this kind of communication, and I have no doubt at all that the psychics I've met who have related their information are really talking with those beyond. Their information usually comes quick with details that one listening might not be interested in but valuable in putting forth a picture of the situation.

For example, at Elaine's Haunted Mansion, Laurie talked about the alcohol in one of the rooms and how the ghosts there advised that it should not have been there. Though Ron specifically began talking about the history of that room and the alcohol storage, Laurie immediately jumped to the next subject without considering what he was saying. The ghosts were now talking about the coldness of the room—something completely different. The ghosts seem to take charge of what she sees and is able to communicate. The living, at this time, do not seem to matter. She's in another realm of seeing at these times. It became so evident that this was the case, I began to look for it—expect it. And those things she said at those times, were very important when I began to pull the facts together to write this book.

I'd seen this same behavior with another psychic investigator I'd worked with while assisting another author and her book. Quick, often unrelated, pieces of data spurting out of the psychic's mouth. The real-time conversations were not like this. In normal conversation, both psychics I'd dealt with talked in normal ways—in sentences, clear and concise. When talking to ghosts the whole concept of conversation changed and there was great description being thrown out. If someone talked while the psychic was getting the ghostly perceptions, they would miss out.

Laurie told me a story about a ghost she'd communicated with and its reason for staying behind in our world.

"The ghost we investigated in Philadelphia was a spirit who could be found upstairs in a girl's room. She said her name was Alice, and I asked her why she was staying here in our realm. She told me that it was because she was a bad daughter. I asked, 'Don't you want to see your mother and father again?' She told me again that she was a bad daughter. She said, 'I don't want to go because I think my mom is going to be real mad at me because when I came to Philadelphia to work, I didn't talk to her anymore. And I know I was supposed to write her and visit her, but I didn't. Then she got sick and she died—I'd never gone back to visit her.'"

This is where ghost psychology comes into play, because, indeed, a ghost investigator or psychic who is able to have actual conversations and interactions with the spirits are often called upon to solve an emotional problem. The thought, according to all investigators I've talked with, is to do what's best for the ghost. Laurie continued to talk with the ghost in the bedroom about her mother and her feelings of fear relating to forgiveness:

> "Well, the mother forgives her and you gotta tell her that. You can kind of feel another presence in the background. I told the girl, 'Your mother is here.' And she said she could see her mother but that she wasn't totally convinced that her mother wasn't angry. I said, 'Your mother loves you. She's not angry with you. She wants to see you again.'
>
> "This is like therapy for ghosts (said in jest). You tell them that the mother wants to see them again. It's the same thing I try to do in some of these houses where someone is hanging around and they really shouldn't be. I tell them that they can be real happy on the other side instead of

*just puttering around here, with us, for eternity—and*
*scaring people when they don't mean to.*

*"I told the girl, 'You can go and be with your mother*
*who loves you and desperately wants to see you again. You*
*said that you're sorry that you never went to see her. She's*
*waiting to see you right now.' The ghost was considering*
*it and told me, 'I'll think about it."*

Laurie then told the ghost that if she found that she
was not happy with the new arrangement, she could
come back. This, then, convinced the ghost—and it
left. Laurie's question was: What did this ghost think
she was gaining by staying? In this case, there was no
gain, rather, the girl was afraid. She didn't want to
face her mother—she was afraid of her and what *might*
happen. "It's like anything that is potentially unpleas-
ant that people want to avoid. The ghosts may know
that they've done something wrong to a particular
person during life and then decide that they are just
going to stay here. And, like I said to this ghost, 'This
is ridiculous. You've been here a hundred years. Just
go.' But I've known some that just aren't going to
go—and I don't try to make them go."

But there *are* issues with doing the right thing for
the ghost when it comes to sending them away! Laurie reminded me that some people do not want their
ghosts gone! And there is anger at a psychic or investigator for assisting with that transition. (It's always best
to know the surrounding circumstances when going

into any investigation or ghostly experience. Ghosts have become good for business and economic growth in an area. And when both sides are happy, don't mess with something that's not broken!)

I was also curious about the actual personalities of the ghosts, since we'd seen quite a few in our research. Laurie said:

> "We don't understand everything in the world. Ghosts were here before we were. To send them away would be like someone coming into my own house and saying, 'leave.' I'd say, 'Yeah, right.' It [the ghost] is like a person without a body. You can talk to it like a person. It has feelings like a person. They can be crazy like a person. They can be angry, sad, happy…crazy is scary, though. Some ghosts are still in the moment of their death, which is upsetting for anyone who is sensitive to it. This is why people sometimes get really scared or upset, and some people start crying because emotions can be projected onto you. They connect with you on that emotion and it completely fills your body. Then you can become terrified and you feel as though you just have to get out of there.

> "Another reason for ghosts to stay that I didn't say earlier: If someone dies and you really love that person and you can't stop thinking about them and you miss them so much—and wish they were back, they can't leave. You won't let go of them. And sometimes, they stay because you are so devastated that they feel bad. Then they will be stuck. So I try to tell people, let go of this person because

*they don't belong here and they need to move on. Nobody can move on as long as the spirit is still here. You're still stuck because you think of them all the time, because they are there with you. And they are stuck here.*

*"They can come back to say hello once in a while. There are whole books written about just that. Sometimes, too, they will come back to help you if something is wrong. And sometimes they come back if something is going on that they don't like. A lot of people note that they show up in their dreams."*

I wondered about those people who either do not believe, don't want to believe, or are terrified to believe in ghosts.

*[About an anonymous incident where a woman was horribly upset at experiencing a ghost] "…She was so upset. I think she thought she was possessed. I didn't want to tell her, but I thought that maybe in her past life she may have been French and that this ghost was able to tap into that part of her, bringing it out. The woman was so upset about it, I didn't want to get into that with her. I just reassured her. 'Did it hurt you; did it follow you home?' 'No, we are fine,' she told me. So I told her not to worry about it. 'Some people would love to have the experience—that's how you have to look at it. Just don't stay there [a bed and breakfast] again. Obviously, the spirit there can make a connection with you and will do it again if you go there—because it wants to talk and obviously had something to say.'*

So, for psychics and ghost investigators, then, there are two very separate kinds of behaviors that they need to be prepared for:

1. Ghostly behavior and the issues that ghosts are trying to deal with. Reasons for their manifestation.

2. Behaviors relating to those living who are experiencing those dead. Is there a welcoming of the experiences or a dread?

Both sides need psychology! I suppose what I'm saying is that anyone wanting to experience the world of ghostly phenomena (in Cape May or anywhere else), it helps to be cognizant of things outside someone's own perceptions.

## Conclusion

So, to wrap things up, I will end as I started: Ghosts are real. Ghosts are quirky. Ghosts are exciting...scary...interesting...intelligent...beyond our understanding.

Oh, and most important—There are ghosts in Cape May. Stop by and say hello to them!

# Bibliography and Resource List

Jordan, Joe J. *Cape May Point, The Illustrated History: 1875 to the Present*. Atglen, Pennsylvania: Schiffer Publishing, 2003.

Marx, Robert. *Shipwrecks in the Americas*. Mineola, New York: Dover Publications, 1983 (Subsequent edition, 1987).

McManus, Craig. *The Ghosts of Cape May*. New Jersey: ChannelCraig Press, 2005.

McManus, Craig. *The Ghosts of Cape May, Book 2*. New Jersey: ChannelCraig Press, 2005.

Roseberry, D. P. *The Ghosts of Valley Forge and Phoenixville*. Atglen, Pennsylvania: Schiffer Publishing, 2007.

Skinner, Tina. *Greetings From Cape May*. Atglen, Pennsylvania: Schiffer Publishing, 2007.

Wright, Jack. *Tommy's Folly*. New Jersey: Beach Plum Press, (Date unknown).

## Website Resources
- Bed and Breakfast Online
www.bbonline.com/nj/windward/history.html

- CapeMay.com
http://www.capemay.com or www.capemay.com/
campemayarchives/2000/ghostsparttwo.html
- The Cape May County Library
www.cape-may.county.lib.nj.us/
- The Greater Cape May Historical Society
http://www.capemayhistory.org/
- Cape May Times Online
http://www.capemaytimes.com/birds/higbee.htm
- Chester County Paranormal Research
Society
http://www.chestercountyprs.com
- CNN Online (Juno—Sea Hunt Inc. 1999)
http://www.cnn.com
- Delaware County Paranormal Research
http://www.delcoghosts.com
- Discover Sea Shipwreck Museum
http://www.discoversea.com/Juno.html
- Haunted New Jersey
http://www.hauntednewjersey.com
- Prints Past. The Southern Mansion.
http://www.printspast.com/selected_print.asp?
PrintID=60280047&Return=architecture-
prints-sloan.htm
- South Jersey Ghost Research Group
www.southjerseyghostresearch.org
- Virginia Business
www.virginiabusiness.com/magazine/yr1999/
aug99/itsup/cover.html

# Appendix

The following information is provided by author and ghost investigator, Fiona Broome and appears in her book, *Ghosts of Austin, Texas*.

For more information, visit http://hollowhill.com/.

## Fiona's Tips for Taking Great Ghost Photos

**Avoid lens flares.** Don't point the lens towards the sun, lights, a full moon, or any reflective surface. At least 80% of the orb photos that I review are clearly reflections from shiny surfaces or lights that are in the frame of the photo or just outside it.

**Don't take pictures in high humidity or rain**. Moisture in the air can result in dozens—even hundreds—of orbs in a single photo. If you see too many orbs in your pictures, or many very tiny orbs among larger ones, they're probably from rain or high humidity.

**Watch out for bugs.** Your ghost hunting companion should watch for insects in front of the camera as you take pictures.

Genuine orbs are almost perfectly round. If the orb is oval, irregularly shaped, or has blurry borders, it's probably an insect.

**Avoid smoke.** Tests show that smoke causes fewer eerie effects than most researchers guessed, smoke. However, even if you can't see or smell it when you're taking your photos—can cause misty figures.

**Keep your camera strap and your hair out of the way.**

**Always take two photos in a row**, moving as little as possible between the clicks of the camera's shutter. If your picture shows an actual anomaly, it will usually appear in only one photo. If it looks almost exactly the same (size, brightness, location) in both pictures, it's probably a reflection, or a hovering insect.

**Save all of your pictures** until you've seen at least a dozen with orbs and anomalies. Until you know what you're looking for, you may not realize how many anomalies are in your photos.

If you use a film camera, the photo lab may adjust the contrast to prevent the orbs (and other anomalies) from "spoiling" your photos. Sometimes, you have to study the negatives to find the orbs.

I've taken hundreds of photos that clearly show orbs on the negative but those same orbs are easily overlooked on the print. It took years of practice to spot these orbs without referring to the negatives.

When you realize how faint some orbs are, you'll probably find dozens of overlooked "ghosts" in your pictures.

◇◇◇◇◇◇◇◇◇◇◇◇◇◇◇◇◇◇◇

# Top Ten Places to Find Ghosts

No matter where you are, certain locations are usually haunted. These sites don't always have ghosts, but they're the best places to start when you're looking for unreported visitors from beyond the grave.

## Theatres

Ghosts frequent places where people have performed on stage. These include movie theatres that were once performance halls.

There are three kinds of ghosts at these locations:

First, at least one actor who is still seen on or near the stage.

Second, a stagehand lingers backstage, usually around the lighting or the curtain controls.

Finally, someone appears towards the back of the hall, especially during rehearsals. He or she almost always smokes a cigarette that people can smell, or they'll see the smoke or the burning ember.

## Battlegrounds

Almost every battleground has some residual energy from the violent and tragic deaths that occurred there. Some battlegrounds are actually haunted by the spirits of the men and women who died there, too. Between Texas' battles for independence, Indian attacks, and Civil War conflicts, you'll find many locations with ghost stories... and real ghosts.

## Cemeteries

It's a cliché but a true one: Ghosts haunt cemeteries. Modern graves—burials that occurred less than fifty years ago—are rarely haunted for very long.

For the most powerful hauntings, look for graves that are at least a hundred years old. Only a few are haunted, but you'll find elevated EMF levels at many of graves, especially if they're unmarked.

## Colleges

Almost every college or university reports at least one ghost. Most also report poltergeist phenomena. The performing arts center is often the most haunted location on campus. In Austin, the University of Texas campus is probably the most haunted college.

## Summer Camps

Most camps—especially Scout camps—have a ghost or two. Usually, these are benevolent ghosts of former camp counselors or the camp manager. An aroma of perfume or pipe smoke is usually reported, related to someone who worked there.

## Very Old, Large Homes and Buildings

Like most ancient castles, many very old, large buildings have ghosts. In an older home, a woman who lived there lingers to be sure that the house and its occupants remain safe. She usually wears a green dress.

Another ghost is mad and lurks in the attic, basement, or an outbuilding. A variation on this is a ghost in the nearby woods or a field next to an old homestead. These hauntings are almost predictable.

## Old Hotels

Many hotels are haunted by the same people who visited them in life. They're usually happy ghosts who return to relax and enjoy themselves.

Classic haunted spots in hotels include the top floor, the elevator, and the lobby. This is true of the Driskill Hotel, Austin's most haunted and elegant hotel, and a favorite destination for visiting ghost hunters.

Around Austin, this category of haunting extends to former brothels. In the late nineteenth century, dozens of feisty, independent-minded madams owned "boarding houses" around downtown Austin. Today, these sites are often clubs, bars, and restaurants in the entertainment and warehouse districts of Austin. And, most of them have great ghost stories to share.

## Hospitals, Retirement Homes, Morgues and Funeral Parlors

As you'd expect, some people aren't willing to leave the last place where they were seen and called by name. However, if these sites are still in use, they're usually off-limits to ghost hunters.

Instead, look for former locations of these kinds of buildings. They're usually haunted by perplexed and sometimes angry ghosts.

Around Austin, there are probably hundreds of unreported ghosts. If you follow these suggestions, you'll find even more ghosts than are included in these pages.

*The following section is provided by the Chester County Paranormal Research Society in Pennsylvania and appears in training materials for new investigators. Please visit www.ChesterCountyprs.com for more information.*

◇◇◇◇◇◇◇◇◇◇◇◇◇◇◇◇

# Glossary

**Air Probe Thermometer**

A thermometer with an external probe that is capable of taking instant measurements of the air temperature.

**Anomalous field**

A field that can not be explained or ruled out by various possibilities, that can be a representation of spirit or paranormal energy present.

**Apparition**

A transparent form of a human or animal, a spirit.

**Artificial field**

A field that is caused by electrical outlets, appliances, etc.

**Aural Enhancer**

A listening device that enhances or amplifies audio signals. i.e., Orbitor Bionic Ear.

**Automatic writing**

The act of a spirit guiding a human agent in writing a message that is brought through by the spirit.

**Base readings**

The readings taken at the start of an investigation and are used as a means of comparing other readings taken later during the course of the investigation.

### Demonic Haunting
A haunting that is caused by an inhuman or subhuman energy or spirit.

### Dowsing Rods
A pair of L-shaped rods or a single Y-shaped rod, used to detect the presence of what the person using them is trying to find.

### Electro-static generator
A device that electrically charges the air often used in paranormal investigations/research as a means to contribute to the materialization of paranormal or spiritual energy.

### ELF
Extremely Low Frequency.

### ELF Meter/EMF Meter
A device that measures electric and magnetic fields.

### EMF
Electro Magnetic Field.

### EVP
Electronic Voice Phenomena.

### False positive
Something that is being interpreted as paranormal within a picture or video and is, in fact, a natural occurrence or defect of the equipment used.

### Gamera
A 35mm film camera connected with a motion detector that is housed in a weather proof container and takes a picture when movement is detected. Made by Silver Creek Industries.

## Geiger Counter

A device that measures gamma and x-ray radiation.

## Infra Red

An invisible band of radiation at the lower end of the visible light spectrum. With wavelengths from 750 nm to 1 mm, infrared starts at the end of the microwave spectrum and ends at the beginning of visible light. Infrared transmission typically requires an unobstructed line of sight between transmitter and receiver. Widely used in most audio and video remote controls, infrared transmission is also used for wireless connections between computer devices and a variety of detectors.

## Intelligent haunting

A haunting of a spirit or other entity that has the ability to interact with the living and do things that can make its presence known.

## Milli-gauss

Unit of measurement, measures in 1000th of a gauss and is named for the famous German mathematician, Karl Gauss.

## Orbs

Anomalous spherical shapes that appear on video and still photography.

## Pendulum

A pointed item that is hung on the end of a string or chain and is used as a means of contacting spirits. An individual will hold the item and let it hang from the finger tips. The individual will ask questions aloud and the pendulum answers by moving.

### Poltergeist haunting

A haunting that has two sides, but same kinds of activity in common. Violent outbursts of activity with doors and windows slamming shut, items being thrown across a room and things being knocked off of surfaces. Poltergeist hauntings are usually focused around a specific individual who resides or works at the location of the activity reported, and, in some cases, when the person is not present at the location, activity does not occur. A poltergeist haunting may be the cause of a human agent or spirit/energy that may be present at the location.

### Portal

An opening in the realm of the paranormal that is a gateway between one dimension and the next. A passageway for spirits to come and go through. See also Vortex.

### Residual haunting

A haunting that is an imprint of an event or person that plays itself out like a loop until the energy that causes it has burned itself out.

### Scrying

The act of eliciting information with the use of a pendulum from spirits.

### Table Tipping

A form of spirit communication, the act of a table being used as a form of contact. Individuals will sit around a table and lightly place there fingertips on the edge of the table and elicit contact with a spirit. The Spirit will respond by "tipping" or moving the table.

## Talking Boards

A board used as a means of communicating with a spirit. Also known as a Quija Board.

## Vortex

A place or situation regarded as drawing into its center all that surrounds it.

## White Noise

A random noise signal that has the same sound energy level at all frequencies.

◇◇◇◇◇◇◇◇◇◇◇◇◇◇◇◇◇◇

# Equipment

In this section, the Chester County Paranormal Research Society looks at the application and benefits of equipment used on investigations with greater detail. The equipment used for an investigation plays a vital role in the ability to collect objective evidence and helps to determine what *is* and *is not* paranormal activity. But a key point to be made here is: the investigator is the most important tool on any investigation. With that said, let us now take a look at the main pieces of equipment used during an investigation...

### The Geiger Counter

The Geiger counter is device that measures radiation. A "Geiger counter" usually contains a metal tube with a thin metal wire along its middle. The space in between them is sealed off and filled with a suitable gas and with the wire at about +1000 volts relative to the tube.

An ion or electron penetrating the tube (or an electron knocked out of the wall by X-rays or gamma rays) tears electrons off atoms in the gas. Because of the high positive voltage of the central wire, those electrons are then attracted to it. They gain energy that collide with atoms and release more electrons, until the process snowballs into an "avalanche", producing an easily detectable pulse of current. With a suitable filling gas, the flow of electricity stops by itself, or else the electrical circuitry can help stop it.

The instrument was called a "counter" because every particle passing it produced an identical pulse, allowing particles to be counted, usually electronically. But it did not tell anything about their identity or energy, except that they must have sufficient energy to penetrate the walls of the counter.

The Geiger counter is used in paranormal research to measure the background radiation at a location. The working theory in this field is that paranormal activity can effect the background radiation. In some cases, it will increase the radiation levels and in other cases it will decrease the levels.

### Digital and 35mm Film Cameras

The camera is an imperative piece of equipment that enabled us to gather objective evidence during a case. Some of the best evidence presented from cases of paranormal activity over the years has been because of photographs taken. If you own your own digital camera or 35mm film camera, you need to be fully aware of what the cameras abilities and limitations are. Digital cameras have been at the center of great debate in the field of paranormal research over the years.

The earlier incarnations of digital cameras were full of inherent problems and notorious for creating "false positive" pictures. A "false positive" picture is a picture that has anomalous elements within the picture that are the result of a camera defect or other natural occurrence. There are many pictures scattered about the internet that claim to be of true paranormal activity, but in fact they are "false positives." Orbs, defined as anomalous paranormal energy that can show up as balls of light or streaks in still photography or video, are the most controversial pictures of paranormal energy in the field. There are so many theories (good and bad) about the origin of orbs and what they are. Every picture in the CCPRS collection that has an orb—or orbs—are not presented in a way that state that they are absolutely paranormal of nature. I have yet to capture an orb photo that made me feel certain that in fact it is of a paranormal nature.

If you use your own camera, understand that your camera is vital. I encourage all members who own their own cameras to do research on the make and model of the camera and see what other consumers are saying about them. Does the manufacturer give any info regarding possible defects or design flaws with that particular model?

Understanding your camera will help to rule out the possibility of interpreting a "false positive" for an authentic picture of paranormal activity.

## Video Cameras

The video camera is also a fundamental tool in the investigation as another way for collecting objective evidence that can support the proof of paranormal activity. The video camera can be used in various ways during the investigation. It can be set on a tripod and left in a location where paranormal activity has been reported. It can also be used as a hand-held camera and the investigator will take it with them during their walk through investigation as a means of documenting to hopefully capture anomalous activity on tape.

Infra-Red technology has become a feature on most consumer level video cameras and depending on the manufacturer can be called "night shot" or "night alive." What this technology does is allow us to use the camera in zero light. Most cameras with this feature will add a green tint or haze to the camera when it is being used in this mode. A video camera with this ability holds great appeal to the paranormal investigator.

## EMF/ELF Meters

EMF = Electro Magnetic Frequency   ELF = Extremely Low Frequency

The EMF/ELF meter is a meter that measures Electric and Magnetic fields in an AC or DC current field. It measures in a unit of measurement called "milli-gauss," named for the famous German mathematician, Karl Gauss. Most meters will measure in a range of 1-5 or 1-10 milli-gauss. The reason that EMF meters are used in paranormal research is because of the theory that a spirit or paranormal energy can add to the energy field when it is materializing or is present in a location. The theory says that, typically, an energy that measures between 3-7 milli-gauss may be of a paranormal origin. This doesn't mean that an artificial field can't also measure within this range. That is why we take base readings and make maps notating where artificial fields occur. The artificial fields are a direct result of electricity, i.e. wiring, appliances, light switches, electrical outlets, circuit breakers, high voltage power lines, sub-stations, etc.

The Earth emits a naturally occurring magnetic field all around us and has an effect on paranormal activity. Geo-magnetic storm activity can also have a great influence on paranormal activity. For more information on this kind of phenomena visit: www.noaa.sec.com.

There are many different types of EMF meters; and each one, although it measures with the same unit of measurement, may react differently. An EMF meter can range from anywhere from $12 to $1,000 or more depending on the quality and features that it has. Most meters are measuring the AC (alternating current, the type of fields created by man-made electricity) fields and some can measure DC (direct current-naturally oc-curring fields, batteries also fall into the category of DC) fields. The benefit of having a meter that can measure DC fields is that they will automatically filter out the artificial fields created by AC fields and can pick up more naturally occurring electro magnetic fields. Some of the higher-tech EMF meters are so sensitive that they can pick up the fields generated by living beings. The EMF meter was originally designed to measure the earth's magnetic fields and also to measure the fields created by electrical an artificial means.

There have been various studies over the years about the long term effects of individuals living in or near high fields. There has been much controversy as to whether or not long term exposure to high fields can lead to cancer. It has been proven though that no matter what, long term exposure to high fields can be harmful to your health. The ability to locate these high fields within a private residence or business is vital to the investigation. We may offer suggestions to the client as to possible solutions for dealing with high fields. The wiring in a home or business can greatly affect the possibility of high fields. If the wiring is old and/or not shielded correctly, it can emit high fields that may affect the ability to correctly notate any anomalous fields that may be present.

## Audio Recording Equipment

Audio recording equipment is used for conducting EVP (Electronic Voice Phenomena) research and experiments. An EVP is a phenomenon where paranormal voices or sounds can be captured with audio recording devices. The theory is that the activity will imprint directly onto the device or tape, but has not been proven to be an absolute fact. The use of an external microphone is essential when conducting EVP experiments with analog recording equipment. The internal microphone on an analog tape recorder can pick up the background noise of the working parts within the tape recorder and can taint the evidence as a whole. Most digital recorders are quiet enough to use the internal microphone, but as a general rule of thumb, we do not use them. An external microphone will be used always. Another theory about EVP research is that an authentic EVP will happen within the range 250-400hz. This is a lower frequency range and isn't easily heard by the human ear, and the human voice does not emit in this range. EVP is rarely heard at the moment it happens—it is usually revealed during the playback and analysis portion of the investigation.

## Thermometers

The use of a thermometer in an investigation goes without saying. This is how we monitor the temperature changes during the course of an investigation. CCPRS is currently using Digital thermometers with remote sensors as a way to set up a perimeter and to notate any changes in a stationary location of an investigation. The Air-probe thermometer can take "real time" readings that are instantly accurate. This is the more appropriate thermometer for measuring air temperature and "cold spots" that may be caused by the presence of paranormal phenomena. The IR Non-contact thermometer is the most misused thermometer in the field of paranormal research. CCPRS does not own or use IR Non-contact thermometers for this reason. The IR (infra-red) Non-contact thermometer is meant for measuring surface temperatures from a remote location. It shoots an infrared beam out to an object and bounces to the unit and gives the temperature reading. I have seen, first hand, investigators using this thermometer as a way to measure air temperature. NO, this is not correct! Enough said. In an email conversation that I have had with Grant Wilson from TAPS, he has said that, "Any change in temperature that can't be measured with your hand is not worth notating…"

Though this Cape May Greetings postcard (cancelled in 1941) welcomes you to a beautiful beach town, that gesture just might include more than you know! So, I bid you Greetings From Haunted Cape May! *Postcard courtesy of the Elwood "Woody" Koch collection*